Praise for Clara Claiborne Park's

Exiting Nirvana
A Daughter's Life with Autism

"An eloquent memoir. . . . A loving and lovely book. . . . Park's analysis of Jessy's seemingly impenetrable systems is fascinating."
—Kevin Riordan, *New Jersey Courier Post*

"As much as *Exiting Nirvana* succeeds in bringing us into the world of autism, perhaps its greater accomplishment is in making us reconsider whatever we thought we knew about what it means to be human in the first place."
—David Royko, *Chicago Tribune*

"This book will help both parents and professionals to have a greater understanding of the mind of a person with autism."
—Temple Grandin, Ph.D., author of
Thinking in Pictures and Other Reports from My Life with Autism

"A fascinating journey into the autistic mind. . . . The anecdotes are compelling, the turns of phrase quite elegant."
—Sara Solovitch, *San Jose Mercury News*

"Immensely readable. . . . A frank, honest telling of how a mother refused to surrender. . . . A unique and invaluable case study of the nature of autism."
—Richard Nunley, *Berkshire Eagle*

"An extraordinarily well-written, moving account of a mother's struggle not only to bring her daughter into the world but also to teach her how to have an extraordinary life. . . . The readership of this book is virtually the universe of readers. Anyone interested in child psychiatry should grab this book immediately. Any parent of a special-needs child of any kind will glean much from this book. Anyone interested in existential questions of being can learn from Clara and Jessy's journey together. I would make this book required reading in the curriculum of every discipline in the mental health field." —Jeffrey L. Geller, M.D., M.P.H., *Psychiatric Services: A Journal of the American Psychiatric Association*

"I adore Clara Park and often reread *The Siege* to maintain my professional focus in times of overwhelming doubt about how to help children and their families. . . . Now she touches my mind, heart, and soul again through her poetic voice in *Exiting Nirvana*. . . . There are insights into autism that can only be gained through the time-honored words of a mother's love." —Kathleen Quill, Ed.D., Director, Autism Institute, and author of *Teaching Children with Autism*

"A masterpiece. Clara Park's earlier book *The Siege* was also a masterpiece, but the two masterpieces are quite different. The first was about childhood. The second about maturity. Now we have prose instead of lyrics, serenity instead of passion. Clara has navigated through the storms and come safe to shore. Her daughter Jessy has grown slowly into self-awareness, and Clara's work is done." —Freeman Dyson, the Institute for Advanced Study, Princeton, and author of *Origins of Life*

"A beautifully written portrait of a little understood illness. . . . Park has told Jessy's story with clear objectivity but also with a mother's warmth, sharing the bewilderment, frustrations, and triumphs of life with an autistic child. A keen observer of detail, she has patiently unraveled many of the mysteries of Jessy's behavior, both for herself and the reader. Though this is a book about Jessy, it's also indirectly about one of Jessy's most fortunate accidents of fate—her remarkable mother." —Donna Marchetti, *Cleveland Plain Dealer*

Exiting Nirvana

A Daughter's Life with Autism

Clara Claiborne Park

Foreword by Oliver Sacks

Little, Brown and Company

Boston   New York   London

By Clara Claiborne Park

The Siege
Rejoining the Common Reader
You Are Not Alone
Exiting Nirvana

Title page: Jessy at age thirty-five. Relaxing at the beach, she practices her "imagery scenes" (chapter 10). Photograph by Rosalie Winard.

Copyright © 2001 by Clara Claiborne Park
Foreword copyright © 2001 by Oliver Sacks

Images by Jessica Park copyright © 2001 by Jessica Park. Reprinted with permission of Jessica Park and The Viewing Room, New York City. All rights reserved.

Originally published in hardcover by Little, Brown and Company, March 2001
First Back Bay paperback edition, March 2002

All illustrations are by Jessy Park.

Picture credits and copyright acknowledgments are on pages 224–225.

Library of Congress Cataloging-in-Publication Data

Park, Clara Claiborne.
Exiting nirvana : a daughter's life with autism / Clara Claiborne Park. — 1st. ed.
p. cm.
Includes bibliographical references.
ISBN:0316691240   ISBN:978-0-316-69124-6
1. Park, Jessy, 1958– 2. Autism — Patients — Biography. 3. Parents
of autistic children — Biography. 4. Autistic children —
Family relationships. I. Title.

RC553.A88 P374 2001
616.89'82'0092 — dc21

[B]   00-033554

10 9 8 7 6 5 4 3 2 1

Q-MART

Book design by Fearn Cutler

Printed in the United States of America

To Jessy,

who once couldn't talk and has spoken so much of this book

And to the memory of Ernest C. Pascucci

Contents

Contents

Foreword

In 1967 a remarkable book was published — *The Siege,* by Clara Claiborne Park, an account of her daughter's first eight years. It was remarkable on several counts: it was the first "inside" (as opposed to clinical) account of an autistic child's development and life; and it was written with an intelligence, a clear-sightedness, an insight, and a love that brought out to the full the absolute strangeness, the "otherness," of the autistic mind. It also brought out how much an empathetic understanding could help to lay siege to autism's seemingly impregnable isolation.

Jessy Park — "Elly," as she was called in *The Siege* — is now past forty, and Clara Park has now given us a sequel that is, to my mind, more remarkable still. *The Siege* could only relate the beginnings of a life, whereas *Exiting Nirvana* gives us a story forty years long, the whole of Jessy's unfolding from the almost mute eight-year-old she was in 1967 to the richly gifted, though still clearly autistic, human being she is today.

Over the years the Parks have studied as well as loved Jessy. They have kept detailed records of every stage of her development — the development of her language, her emotions, her interests and moods; of her capacities (or incapacities) for understanding other people, the social world; of her capacities for logical and systematic thought; and, not least, of her varied and singular (and sometimes hugely complex) obsessions and "systems." There is more "data" on Jessy, I suspect, than on any other autistic human being who has ever lived. And from this richness, Clara Park — a superb observer no less than a devoted parent — has distilled a lucid and beautifully wrought narrative, full not only of her own deep observations and thoughts, but of poignant and funny anecdotes of every kind ("A book should consist of *examples*," wrote Wittgenstein), and the strange, mad poetry of Jessy's own words. It reveals the life and mind and world of an autistic person with a depth and detail never before achieved.

It shows, too, how at least some of what might be called the defects or strangenesses of autism can also become singular strengths. Jessy is incapable of lying, or of detecting lies; the concept of deceit is unavailable to her. She herself is such an innocent that she cannot comprehend the concept of innocence. She is extremely literal-minded. She was wholly incapable at first — though is now capable to a small degree — of putting herself in others' shoes, of sensing their positions or perspectives, for it seems to be of the essence with Jessy, as with all autistic people, that she is "mind-blind," or lacking in so-called theory of mind.

Jessy has been subject, from an early age, to sudden enthusiasms (her word) or obsessions (the medical word, which she has happily embraced), going from numbers and colors and unusual sounds and words to radio dials and heaters, to certain roads and houses, to atmospheric anomalies and the night sky. These obsessions, elaborated by an incessantly active and systematizing mind, have led Jessy to construct amazingly intricate systems in which weather, mood, flavors, colors — a dozen variables — are all interconnected and correlated with one another. (Jessy can instantly learn a word like "correlation," because this is already a concept she possesses, when, in contrast, she cannot read the expressions on people's faces, or the intentions in their voices, cannot comprehend why she cannot instantly evict someone from a restaurant table she considers "hers," and is generally blind to all social meanings.) Though idiosyncratic, Jessy's systems bring to mind the elaborate, pseudoscientific systems of numerology and astrology.

In the past twenty years, Jessy's obsessions have been transformed, or transmuted, into paintings — paintings, at first, of radio dials and heaters (very fresh, brilliantly colored, a sort of Pop Art), and now exquisite paintings of houses and churches, in which an uncanny accuracy of line is combined with colors of surreal brilliance. Night scenes are her favorites, in which buildings stand out incandescently against a dark sky — cobalt, or ultramarine, or (her favorite) "purplish black" — and in which every major star is portrayed in its exact position and magnitude.

Exiting Nirvana is never sentimental, but it is often lyrical, and even allegorical in the universality of its themes. All of us, perhaps, have to move from some primal Eden of self-sufficiency, self-absorption, changelessness, timelessness, into the vicissitudes and frustrations and unpredictabilities of the world, into a life that may be full of growth and adventure, but that threatens continual contingency and risk. It may be — this is certainly a central theme of the book — that this sort of Nirvana can achieve in the autistic an overwhelming, engulfing, annihilating intensity, shutting out the world, in effect, by a timeless absorption in monotonous and repeated activities. Clara Park, in some of the most memorable passages of *The Siege,* described just this with the eighteen-month-old Jessy; and Temple Grandin (who in referring to her own autism once called herself an "anthropologist on Mars") tells us how she too as a child would "sit on the beach for hours dribbling sand through my fingers and fashioning miniature mountains," blind to the human beings, the human activities and interactions, all about her. We have all, perhaps, dribbled sand in this way, but for the autistic there is a very real danger that such dribbling will engross an entire lifetime. It was this sort of enraptured, timeless, self-stimulating nothingness that Jessy's parents had to put under siege in the first place. But then the siege became a journey into the possibilities of coexisting in our world, partly by understanding it (which is still possible for Jessy only to a very limited extent), more by learning its (to her unintelligible) rules and customs and values by rote, while at the same time keeping, even strengthening, her own autistic singularity and identity — that immediacy and purity and simplicity of mind which lies at the core of her character and art.

Though Jessy cannot live independently (and never will be able to), and though she requires supervision at work, she does work, with extreme competence and absolute reliability, as a mail clerk. She balances her checkbook; she pays taxes; and (the most difficult, perhaps, for anyone who is autistic) she has come to appreciate something of the feeling of other people, other minds, and of the nature of friends and friendship. And if she has left or renounced Nirvana to some extent, she can recapture it in the stillness, the timelessness, the beauty of her strange paintings. This may, indeed, be as crucial in balancing her life as anything else.

For many years autism was seen as a defensive withdrawal from the world, on the part of a child neglected and alienated by cold, remote parents — Leo Kanner, who identified the condition and named it, spoke of "refrigerator mothers." But there is nothing whatever to support such a notion and everything to

refute it. Jessy, the "baby" of her family, has been dearly loved —
not only by her parents, but by her siblings — since birth; has perhaps had *less* trauma than most of us; and gives the impression,
for much of the time, of an odd (and, as it were, secret) happiness.
Clara Park speaks here of Jessy's continuing capacity for "autistic
delight":

> Once she'd exult over her discovery that "70003 is a prime!". . .
> Then her interest subsided; other things evoked her secret
> smile. Stars. Rainbows. Clouds. Weather phenomena. Quartz
> heaters. Odometers. Streetlamps. A strange procession of
> obsessions, for a year or two eliciting an intensity of emotion
> approaching ecstasy, then subsiding into mere pleasure.
> Wordless once, now a word, a phrase, could thrill her.
> "Asteroid explosion," "digital fluorescent number change."

The obverse of this — and now much rarer — is the piercing
cry of desolation that Jessy sometimes emits. The causes of these,
Clara Park writes, were

> as inexplicable as the causes of her delight. Perhaps her
> milk was served in a glass instead of her silver cup. . . .
> Perhaps one of the six washcloths in the family bathroom
> was missing. . . . Even when she began to put words
> together . . . we were no nearer understanding. It was, we
> could be sure, never anything that would make another
> child shriek, it was always trivial, what normal people
> would call trivial — trivial in everything but its effect on
> Jessy. . . . By the time she was twelve or thirteen, she *could*
> tell us. But what good did it do to know that a lighted win-
> dow had disrupted the darkness of the building across the

street, that a cloud had covered the moon, that she had accidentally caught sight of Sirius . . . ?

These sudden raptures or desolations, though occurring in such trivial (but to her passionately charged) contexts, bring to mind some of the raptures and distresses that creative artists and scientists sometimes have — the ecstatic "Eureka!" of discovery or insight, the sudden feeling of calamity when things do not go right. This is all infinitely far from the emotional dullness, or muting, or "indifference," that is sometimes ascribed to the autistic.

Clara Park speaks of Jessy's strange happiness as characteristic of her condition. I am not sure that this is so — that autism *alone* can generate such a temperament or disposition or life-mood. Knowing the Parks somewhat, I can perhaps say what Clara Park herself is too modest to say: that this is a most extraordinary family — the mother a gifted teacher and writer, the father a theoretical physicist, and Jessy's three older siblings intellectually gifted and accomplished. The Park household is one where eager interest and attention turn in all directions, and where intellectual play and fun are the constant atmosphere. And this is not only a creative and playful family, but a deeply supportive and loving one. Surely some of Jessy's happiness and confidence, and the diversity of her own interests, must reflect this rare family situation.

Most books about a "condition" or an "afflicted person" are sad if not tragic, even if they strike a note of heroism or bravery. *Exiting Nirvana* is a great exception, for while it is as deep and unsparing as reality itself, it has a joyous and lyrical quality from beginning to end.

Oliver Sacks
January 2001

Exiting Nirvana

Jessy Park: *Judy's House in
Hastings-on-Hudson,* 1996.

CHAPTER I

Introductory

How to begin? In bewilderment, I think — that's the truest way. That's where we began, all those years ago. That's where everyone begins who has to do with autistic children. And even now, when my daughter is past forty . . .

This morning, at breakfast, Jessy reports an exciting discovery. It's a word. She doesn't say it quite clearly, but it's recognizable: "remembrance." "A new fluffy-in-the-middle! Found in the newspaper! It *is* fluffy in the middle!" Her voice is triumphant, her face is alight. "I *saw* one! With five on each side!" Leave that unexplained, in all its strangeness. For now. Shift to something less bizarre. Somewhat less bizarre.

.   .   .

Jessy is painting a church. Her acrylics are neatly arranged on the table beside her. With her sable brush and steady hand she has rendered every brick, every curlicue of the Corinthian capital, every nick and breakage in the old stone, accurately, realistically, recognizably. Except that the capital is a vivid, penetrating, astonishing

3

green. The elaborate details of the stonework are picked out in shade upon shade of rose and violet and turquoise and ultra-marine and yellow and green, a different green. The tower thrusts upward into azure sky. Into the blue (five shades, she tells me) she's introduced three zigzags, one above another, exactly parallel, zig for zag. Lightning, she says. She's painted lightning before, realistically, recognizably, working from photographs, since lightning, unlike a church, doesn't hold still for her to sketch it. But no one ever photographed lightning like this, so neatly angular, so controlled. "I invented it!" Happily she explains: it's what she sees when she has one of her brief migraine episodes. Migraine can be painless; Jessy is quite comfortable with hers. She points out that the zigzags too are colored: "Very pale mint, lavender, and yellow."

Very pale; to me they all look white. Only a scrutiny as sharp as Jessy's would notice a difference between them. Only a mind as free of conventional perceptions would make lightning out of a migraine illusion, or convert the dramatic disorder of nature into this orderly vision, or transfigure a deteriorating church with colors beyond the rainbow. Bizarre becomes original in the language of art, becomes surreal.

．　．　．

But Jessy's life, and life with Jessy, is not all strangeness. Indeed, it is less strange every year, more ordinary, more like other people's lives. We work, we shop, we do errands. So consider this recent incident, at the little post office on the island where we spend our summers. The parking lot is full. I'll park at the curb and rush inside while she waits in the car.

She doesn't like that. "We could ask someone to move so we can park," she says.

"We can't do that," I tell her.

She confirms this. "We can't ask them because they were there first." She was just hoping; she really does know the rule. She learned it years ago, when she asked some people to move from her favorite table and had to leave the restaurant. Now I counter-sink the lesson: "How would you feel if someone asked us to move so they could park?"

"Hurt my *feelings*."

Still, evidently, more work to be done. "No, it wouldn't hurt your feelings. Feelings get hurt when somebody does something or says something and you think they don't like you. Or criticize you." (This is getting complicated.) "It's not when they do something *you* don't like; then you get *irritated,* or *angry*. That's different."

That was a year ago. This week, at the supermarket, the lesson resurfaces. Near the checkout, I've met a friend; we get talking. Too long, thinks Jessy; the shopping's done, time to go. She waits a minute, two, then pushes our friend's cart with an abruptness just on the edge of aggression. She's caught herself, but she knows she's been rude. Later, as we talk it over, she plugs in the familiar, all-purpose phrase: "Hurt his feelings." Has there been any progress at all?

I begin to correct her. But she anticipates me. "Not hurt his feelings, *irritated!*" She remembered! This is the first time she's ever made the distinction. Except, except . . . except that he wasn't irritated. He's known Jessy from childhood, and makes allowances. How to explain *that* and still convey the necessity of self-control? Words, feelings, contexts, human meanings. We'll be working on these for years to come.

·   ·   ·

Forty years. The middle of the journey. The middle of her journey; nearer the end of mine. But I had better begin nearer the beginning, where I began thirty-four years ago, when I first realized there was a story to tell.

> *We start with an image — a tiny, golden child on hands and knees, circling round and round a spot on the floor in mysterious, self-absorbed delight. She does not look up, though she is smiling and laughing; she does not call our attention to the mysterious object of her pleasure. She does not see us at all. She and the spot are all there is, and though she is eighteen months old, an age for touching, tasting, pointing, pushing, exploring, she is doing none of these. She does not walk, or crawl up stairs, or pull herself to her feet to reach for objects. She doesn't want any objects. Instead, she circles her spot. Or she sits, a long chain in her hand, snaking it up and down, up and down, watching it coil and uncoil, for twenty minutes, half an hour, longer . . .*[1]

It was like that; that was when we began to know.

.   .   .

To know what? Today, any reasonably savvy pediatrician would know what, would recognize autism when she saw it in as pure a form as this. Autism is when your two-year-old looks straight through you to the wall behind — you, her mother, her father, sister, brother, or anybody else. You are a pane of glass. Or you are her own personal extension, your hand a tool she uses to get the cookie she will not reach for herself. Autism is when your three-year-old sorts her blocks by shape and color so you can't think she's retarded. Autism is when your eight-year-old fills a carton with three-quarter-inch squares of cut-up paper to sift between her fingers for twenty minutes, half an hour, longer. Autism is when your eleven-year-old fills sheet after sheet with division, division by 3, by 7, 11, 13, 17, 19. . . . But that's enough, there are many books about autism now, anyone can read the symptoms. I need the image for what the symptoms don't convey: this child was *happy*. Is it not happiness to want nothing but what you have? Craving, the Buddha taught, is the source of all suffering, detachment the road to the serene equilibrium of Nirvana.

. . .

But Nirvana at eighteen months? *That's too soon.*

. . .

Yet I must start with that happiness, if only because, in those bad years, it was so thoroughly denied. Only in a few psychoanalytic backwaters is it still believed that the autistic child, like the so-called zombies of the concentration camps, is withdrawing from unbearable agony. This now discredited notion was once widely accepted, thanks to the journalistic skills of Bruno Bettelheim. "Autistic children . . . fear constantly for their lives," he wrote. "The precipitating factor in infantile autism is the parent's wish that his child should not exist."[2] His? The sentence comes from a section headed "The Mother in Infantile Autism." I could quote more, but I won't. It is painful to return to the book Bettelheim, with his gift for metaphor, called *The Empty Fortress* — and thank God and the rules of evidence, it has become unnecessary. Autism is now almost universally recognized as a developmental disorder, multiply caused: genetic predisposition, pre- or postnatal viral infection, chromosomal damage, biological agents still unknown. Magnetic resonance imaging shows brain anomalies. So do autopsies. The research goes on. Every bit of it, however little it can as yet contribute to our own child's habilitation — unlike Bettelheim, we do not speak of cure — buries deeper the injustice of that terrible accusation.

For Jessy was happy, happy circling, happy sifting, happy dividing. Her happiness was not occasional or accidental, it was characteristic of her condition, as characteristic, as needful to acknowledge, as the eerie banshee shrieks and wails that the books call tantruming, but which no parent of a normal toddler would confuse with the familiar noise of a child who's not getting what it wants. This was not anger or frustration, this was desolation, a desolation as private, as enveloping, as her happiness.

What precipitated it? The causes were as inexplicable as the causes of her delight. Perhaps her milk was served in a glass instead of her silver cup, or offered after the meal instead of before. Perhaps she couldn't find a particular square — she could identify it — among those thousands of bits of paper. Perhaps one of the six washcloths in the family bathroom was missing, or three, or two; she knew how many, though she had no words for number. Speechless, she gave no clue. Even when she began to put words together, years later, we were no nearer understanding. It was, we could be sure, never anything that would make another child shriek, it was always trivial, what normal people would call trivial — trivial in everything but its effect on Jessy. How long would the sounds continue? Ten minutes (if we could guess the cause and rectify it), half an hour, one hour, two? By the time she was twelve or thirteen she *could* tell us. But what good did it do to know that a lighted window had disrupted the darkness of the building across the street, that a cloud had covered the moon, that she had accidentally caught sight of Sirius, that she had been waylaid on the street by a manhole cover bearing the word "water"? "Water," it turned out, was "fluffy in the middle." Ten years later she was happy to explain: "At least two small letters on each side, but even. With one tall letter. Bothered me to see it for about two weeks and then went away and bothered me to hear it for I *think* about a semester and then went away." Why did it bother her? "Combination of fluffy in the middle and liquid and part of the car. In the radiator. Only bad if a combination of three. That called the forbidden combination." All clear now?

But it was not such distress that defined her. It came, it passed, it was *over,* its transitoriness as mysterious as its intensity. Next day it could become a subject of cheerful conversation — next day, or ten years later. "No *wonder* I cried!" she'll say, her voice alive with her characteristic rising, positive, happy intonation.

She is happy still. I can't think of another woman in her forties who is more content with who she is, less likely to question how she lives or what she does. Though she no longer circles a spot or snakes a chain up and down, she still has her sources of strange, private pleasure. Things once bad may even become good, as has happened with fluffy-in-the-middle words. Last year she was delighted to find "nuclear" and "nucleus" to add to a list including "radio," "valve," "molar" ("I saw that on June '91"), and "unwelcome." And now, "remembrance."

It is, however, far more important that over the years such mysterious pleasures — and pains — have been joined by others more "normal," more recognizable to other human beings, more *connected* to other human beings, as she has learned, slowly and imperfectly, to function not only beside them but with them, in a shared world. That is her achievement, made possible (like all the achievements of profoundly handicapped people) by the work and support of many others — young people who lived with us and became wise and resourceful therapists; patient teachers;

accepting, helpful people in her workplace and her community. And always, first and last, her family — ourselves, her mother and father, with whom she still lives, and her sisters and brother. That is what this forty-year journey has been about.

It has not been about a miraculous recovery, though selective narration could give that illusion. It has not been about happiness either; in very real ways it has been about its opposite. It has been about growth, and there is no growth in Nirvana. The world we share, the only world we had to offer that wordless baby, is our common world of risk, frustration, loss, of unfulfilled desire as well as of activity and love. We could not leave Jessy to her empty serenity. We would not, as was often recommended in those days, institutionalize her "for the sake of the other children," to spend her days somewhere in a back ward, rocking. We would keep her with us, entice, intrude, enter where we were not wanted or needed.

It was like assaulting a walled city. I called my book about it *The Siege,* choosing the title two years before I'd ever heard of an empty fortress. The metaphor is that strong. Four years, five years, six years — we did get into the walled city. But of course when she began to look at us, to recognize us, to need us — even, in her way, to love us — this was no goal achieved but only a beginning. The siege metaphor became transmuted into a more ordinary one. Siege into journey.

. . .

When Jessy was small there were no real explanations for the condition Leo Kanner, the noted child psychiatrist, had identified in 1943 and called Early Infantile Autism. He had observed and described those eerily detached children; he had thought that such a profound inability to relate to others was probably "innate."

But he had also speculated in a different direction; the phrase "refrigerator parents" was also his. Twenty-five years later, before the newly formed National Society for Autistic Children (now Autism Society of America), he would repudiate this explanation in words none of us who heard him would ever forget: "Herewith I especially acquit you people as parents." But though he called *The Empty Fortress* "the empty book," the ghost of parental responsibility was not so easily laid to rest.[3] Nor was there as yet research to offer convincing support for alternative hypotheses.

In the more than thirty years since then, evidence has accumulated for more merciful — and realistic — explanations. Suppose an impairment in what we now call information processing. A new baby is flooded with information — what William James called a "buzzing, blooming confusion" of light, shadow, color, sound, constantly changing. And if this baby's brain is not ready to do what other babies do so naturally that we don't even think about it, to make sense of that confusion of sense impressions, to resolve it into what it can recognize as faces, voices, which experience can render familiar and welcome? What then? Suppose she cannot do what other babies do instinctively, understand the changing expressions on those faces, the tones of those voices. Might she not prefer the security of a world she *could* make sense of, a world that didn't change, or changed predictably — a world not of faces, not of voices, certainly not of words, but of spots on the floor and snaking chains? Of clear, unchanging, identifiable shapes and colors? And when that secure order was disrupted, might she not be desolate?

Supplement this with another conceptualization. When the anthropologist Clifford Geertz summarizes "the critical features of human thinking," he does not jump forward to what we might be expecting: sequencing of events, perception of cause and effect, induction and deduction. What he lists is far more fundamental: "joint attention with others to objects and actions, attribution of beliefs, desires, and emotions to others, grasping the general significance of situations."[4] Shall we call this, with the British specialist Uta Frith, a "theory of mind"? It seems too grand a phrase to describe what little tiny average babies, as soon as they are born, get busy developing. Yet these are the skills, this is the natural human knowledge without which the social world, that interwoven tissue of meanings into which every baby is plunged, is unintelligible.

These conceptualizations were not available when Jessy circled her spot; now we see how well they explain the challenges she, and we, lived with. For overwhelmingly these challenges were social. As she grew, we were to discover how little trouble Jessy had with sequencing, cause and effect, induction and deduction. But "joint attention"? It is such a simple thing. A mother and a baby look at a picture book together. The mother points; soon the baby will too. Or they play clap hands or peekaboo; mother and baby laugh. Yet learning cannot take place without these "critical features of human thinking." We learn by imitation; imitation is a social act. It does not occur in Nirvana, where there is neither need nor opportunity for joint attention.

. . .

By the time Jessy was six and seven she could put two or three words together; she heard, even understood a little of what we said to her. How could we teach her to understand more, speak more intelligibly? Further, how could we motivate her to do the simple activities it became clear she was capable of doing? She could count, even subtract; the washcloth anxiety proved that.

She could notice the slightest deviation from a pattern. Clearly she could set the table. But why should she? To imitate her sisters? To please her mother? Such natural, social motivators are meaningless without "attribution of beliefs, desires, and emotions to others," without a "theory of mind." At two and a half she had drawn a closed circle, an X, even, astonishingly, a J. *Once;* six months later she wouldn't even pick up a crayon. Why should she? Why should anybody do anything? She could distinguish the most subtle shades of color; she did not utter her first adjectives until six, but when they came they were not the commonplace "bad" or "nice," laden with social value. Rather (of two VW's side by side) she chirped, cheerfully, positively, correctly, "Peacock BLUE car, peacock GREEN car!" Yet later, after I had lured her back into drawing, she would take the first crayon available. Yellow on white? Why not? She drew for her own purposes, not to be visible to others. Sometimes she would even cut up what she had drawn, to join the other three-quarter-inch squares in her sifting carton.

Colors were easy. Numbers, even arithmetical processes, were easy. They were there in her head already, waiting for names. The year she turned nine we sat together as I filled sheet after sheet with rows of renditions of valentine heart-candies, things she knew and liked. They could be counted, grouped in twos, threes ... fives ... nines ... which could themselves be grouped: three groups of nine heart-candies clearly made twenty-seven. Or I drew circles and divided them into halves, thirds, fourths, fifths — fractions! Or I added pentagons and hexagons to the triangles and squares she'd recognized before she was three. With her still rudimentary speech she asked for the series to continue: "Seven sides? Eight sides?" Heptagon, octagon, dodecagon — she learned *those* words as soon as I spoke them. We could share attention when I entered her world, an abstract world of order, repetition, all that represented intelligibility, security, in the bewilderment of talk she could not understand, body language she could not read, social clues she could not interpret. Two years later she would spend hour upon hour in solitary, not to say compulsive, multiplying and dividing. We watched her cover sheet after sheet with divisions by 7, 11, 13, 17, 19, identifying primes and prime factors, happy in a world of number.

Jessy still retains her capacity for autistic delight. What makes her happy today? Once she'd exult over her discovery that "70003 is a *prime!*" Then numbers became what she calls "too good," so good that she would speak them only in whispers, or refuse to say them at all. Then her interest subsided; other things evoked her secret smile. Stars. Rainbows. Clouds. Weather phenomena. Quartz heaters. Odometers. Streetlamps. A strange procession of obsessions, for a year or two eliciting an intensity of emotion approaching ecstasy, then subsiding into mere pleasure. Wordless once, now a word, a phrase, could thrill her. "Asteroid explosion," "digital fluorescent number change." Recently it's anything to do with banks, checks, above all, *fees*. "There's a fee in feeling! And feet!" We know that special smile, that faraway gaze. But don't, don't ask her, "Why are you smiling?" The phrase itself (and there are others) invites desolation, the banshee wail; we don't know why. Was she punished at school for daydreaming? Does she resent the invasion of her secret world? She won't say. Could she if she would?

What's an obsession in psychiatry becomes in art the exploration of a theme. We encourage her to paint these sources of delight. They make her painting not a task but a pleasure, and infuse it with the surreality of her secret world. Though people buy her paintings, there's one she hasn't wanted to sell. It's up in her room, a rendition, in lovely pastels, of the two best things in all of New York City, marvelously come together in the atrium of the World Financial Center: the Merrill Lynch bull and the logo of Godiva chocolates. Though her own script is that of an unusually neat third-grader, the elegant lettering is perfectly reproduced, with her unerring hand and eye. Godiva, Merrill Lynch. The very words make her smile.

We encourage her obsessions in paintings, but we must limit them in daily life. Fascinated at first, people can enjoy just so much conversation about fees, and they may actively object if Jessy scrutinizes their bank statements. We have made sacrifices for the precious ordinariness of habilitation. Would Jessy's mathematical obsession, properly nurtured, have made her into a computer whiz? I doubt it. Her calculations led nowhere; she was interested in doing them, repeating them, contemplating them, not in using them. Her math is now limited to her bank book and her tax forms, her division of the weekly grocery bill, her unerring memory for the mailbox numbers of students who graduated years ago. Numbers, once so absorbing, have gone to join her spot. So have the "little imitation people." (Long ago, when we looked at the illustrated *Gulliver's Travels,* "Lilliputian" must have sounded like that to her.) Once they peopled the appliances, a family in each. Yet are they really gone? I ask her today: Are they still around, perhaps in the office computer? She says they are, but she won't talk about them as she used to. And she's smiling her secret smile.

· · ·

Everybody likes to be astonished. Astonishing abilities and strange preoccupations have become part of the lore of autism, though many autistic people do not have them. "Savant skills" they're called today, our kindly vocabulary of sensitivity having jettisoned the old term "idiot savant." But "savant" has a hollow ring to the parents of a child to whom algebraic processes make more sense than the social interactions of Dick, Jane, and Sally. The challenges of daily life are less interesting to read about, and much more important. Jessy had to learn, if she could, to listen, to speak, to understand, even to read and write, all of those being part of daily life in the twentieth century. In time she did, as she learned to feed herself, to dress herself, to use the toilet, to make her bed, to perform useful tasks about the house. I do not write "make herself useful": to do that you have to perceive the desires and emotions of others, and the achievement of joint attention was not enough to call that skill into being. But concrete skills were not difficult to acquire once she learned to imitate. The much-maligned techniques of behavior modification — rewards and more rarely penalties — eventually provided her adequate motivation. Characteristically, the reinforcers were not food or praise but numbers, a rising tally on a golf counter. Every new skill made life easier for us and richer for her, as her repertoire of activities expanded.

But the most important skills are social. Jessy's social understanding remained, and remains, radically incomplete. Such simple lessons. "We can't ask them to move because they were there first." The difference between irritation and hurt feelings. Making sense of people, "grasping the general significance of situations." What the autistic adult, like the autistic child, finds hardest of all.

What is it like to have a mind that picks "remembrance" out of the newspaper yet must struggle to comprehend the most ordinary vocabulary of social experience? What is it like to have to learn the myriad rules of human interaction by rote, one by one? By rote, because the criterion of "how would I feel if" is unavailable, since so much of what pleases (or distresses) her does not please others, and so little of what pleases (or distresses) others pleases her. Jessy cannot tell us. Temple Grandin, who emerged from autism to become a professor of animal science at Colorado State University, can articulate concepts unavailable to Jessy; she says being autistic is like being an anthropologist on Mars. Autism, like other biological conditions, comes in varying degrees of severity; Temple's journey has taken her farther than Jessy's ever will. In the course of it she has recognized the necessity of learning to live like the natives. The truest learning is reciprocal: the natives too have a lot to learn.

PART ONE

Talking

"thank you," I whispered

CHAPTER 2   "That is not sound"

In 1961, when we first heard of autism, Jessy was three and a half. Our doctor had suspected something wrong at twenty-two months, but hospital examination could find nothing specific. That was not surprising; few were aware of autism then, even within the medical profession. Though Kanner had named it in 1943, and described it with uncanny accuracy, it remained little known, an obscure and rare disorder. Year after year the same figures were repeated: four in ten thousand, two in ten thousand — who knew, really? Who was counting such children? How many doctors were even able to recognize the condition, to distinguish it from all the other possibilities — retardation, aphasia, even, in the early years of a speechless child, deafness? Diagnosis was even more unlikely with children who were not speechless, whose intellectual development seemed to progress normally, yet who shared the characteristic social deficits and odd preoccupations of autism — children like Temple Grandin.

Today such people are more likely to be identified, perhaps as children, perhaps as adolescents or adults. Temple calls herself autistic, but increasingly people like her receive a less daunting diagnosis, Asperger's syndrome, after Hans Asperger, who in Vienna in 1944, quite independently of Kanner, identified this high-functioning variant. Like other biologically based conditions, autism has fuzzy margins. Many parents today must try to make sense of a diagnosis of PDD-NOS, Pervasive Developmental Disorder Not Otherwise Specified, a convenient if uncommunicative label for a child who has a significant number of the symptoms of "classic" autism, but lacks others. (See Appendix II, the DSM IV definition.) Most specialists today would agree with the British psychiatrist Lorna Wing, herself a parent of an autistic daughter, that there is a "continuum of impairments," an autistic spectrum.

> The continuum ranges from the most profoundly physically and mentally retarded person, who has social impairment as one item among a multitude of problems, to the most able, highly intelligent person with social impairment in its subtlest form as his only disability. It overlaps with learning disabilities and shades into eccentric normality. . . . Language, nonverbal communication, reading, writing, calculation, visuo-spatial skills, gross and fine motor-coordination . . . may be intact or delayed or abnormal to any degree of severity in socially impaired people. Any combination of skills and disabilities may be found and any level of overall intelligence.[1]

No wonder the count is uncertain.

Nevertheless, within these variations there is a core, what Wing calls a "triad of impairments" — in social interaction, in communication, and in imaginative activity.[2] The American Psychiatric Association adds another: "restricted repetitive and stereotyped patterns of behavior, interests, and activities."[3] Autism can now be recognized as a worldwide disorder; there are autism societies, mostly started by parents, in India, Thailand, Japan, in Australia, in Africa, in South America, all over Europe. And with better diagnosis, it appears that autism is not even particularly rare. Studies abroad suggest that the incidence of autistic spectrum disorders "may be three to five times higher than the rates found in studies conducted in the U.S. 15–20 years ago, as high as ten to twenty per ten thousand."[4] A recent report from the U.S. Centers for Disease Control on autism in one New Jersey county finds evidence for an even higher figure: 4 per thousand for "strictly defined" autism, 6.7 per thousand when PDD-NOS and Asperger's syndrome are included.[5] This is significantly higher than the incidence of Down syndrome, one of the commonest mental disabilities. It seems likely that every one of us has encountered someone with autism.

The count is uncertain; the future of each child is uncertain too. We have learned a lot since the early days when the Dutch psychiatrist Van Krevelen could describe autistic children as "alike as two raindrops." Those who, like Jessy, have all the "classic" symptoms do indeed look much alike when they are very little; they are much less alike as they grow. Nor does the severity of their symptoms as toddlers necessarily predict where they will fall on the autistic continuum as adolescents and adults; some who, like Temple, have achieved advanced degrees started out very much like Jessy, and some who functioned much better as children have never been able to hold a job. Many autistic children never acquire useful language; some never learn to speak at all. Yet even these may still possess the "splinter skills," the bewildering "islets of intelligence" that set autism apart from the conventional picture of retardation — may discriminate shapes and colors, as Jessy did, or astonish their parents by playing a melody on the family piano. Wherever they fall on the spectrum, however, they will be in need — of skilled teaching as children, and as adolescents and adults, of informed, continuing assistance in coping with social demands that grow more complex the more successfully they enter the normal world.

. . .

That's enough. It's not my intention to survey what's known about autism. There are many people better qualified to do that; I've listed some of their books at the back of this one. It's the experience of autism that I can write about — the initial bewilderment, and the slow growth of at least partial understanding. Indeed there is much to be learned from these strangers. They challenge us to perceive differently, think differently, feel differently, to stretch our imaginations to apprehend, even appreciate, an alternative world. Jessy's journey has led her out of that world — I have called it Nirvana — into the uncertain world of human beings. For that to happen, we too had to travel, as best we could, into experience as foreign to us as ours was to her, learning different things, but learning them together. I would not want to guess who has profited more.

. . .

A description of autism must be anecdotal; without anecdotes there are words but not experience. Anecdotes must temper our yen for the miraculous, keep the account honest. Without them, Jessy's slow progress takes on too much of the aura of the success story everybody wants to hear. Suppose I say what is entirely true: that she has worked, rapidly and efficiently, for twenty years in the mailroom of Williams College, Williamstown, Massachusetts; that she is hardly ever absent and never late; that she pays taxes; that she keeps her bank account accurately to the penny; that she's saved more money than any of her siblings; that increasingly she keeps house for her aging parents. That I haven't touched a vacuum cleaner in years. That she does the laundry, the ironing, some of the cooking, all of the baking. That she is a contributing member of her community and of her family. Who wouldn't hear, behind those words, others: "miracle," "recovery," "cure"? Reality escapes between the lines. Anecdotes must recapture it, as many as I can cram into these pages, not for decoration or liveliness, but for truth.

In our kitchen — where we eat, talk, work, watch TV, where so many things happen — there is a folder filled with envelopes, and a pen kept handy. Inside the envelopes are bits of paper, slips I grab when Jessy does something, says something, that shows progress toward our world, demonstrates a new receptiveness, a new interest, a new understanding, or (the other side of the coin) that reveals how different her experience remains. A few years ago I felt the need of classification; hence the envelopes. Each is labeled with a category: Hypersensitivities; Obsessions; Compulsions (Order, Errors); Verbal; Social; Self-Awareness; Strangeness/Secret Life; Correlations/Analogies; Numbers. It's an odd list, its oddness itself perhaps the best testimony to the oddness it's trying to grasp with these categories that overlap, bleed into each other, provide their multiple takes on the same condition. Now, as I shuffle the slips, I feel them reconfiguring themselves, the fattest envelopes leading the way. I can see I really have only three main categories: Language (imagine, once she couldn't talk, couldn't understand), Social Understanding and Behavior (once there wasn't any), and Strangeness. No one is independent of any other. Hypersensitivities and Obsessions and Compulsions affect

Social Behavior, they intensify Strangeness. Jessy's Analogies and Correlations are extremely Strange; so are her Numbers. Her Language reflects it all. As in this anecdote — what happened the morning of October 7, 1973, when Jessy, fifteen years old, made herself eight pieces of bacon.

> *Why eight? I asked.*
> "Because of good."
> *?*

I transcribe from my notes. Though it would make for a neater narrative, I won't reinvent the words of the question I didn't record. My question mark, floating in blankness, is a truer rendition.

> "Because Ann cough and burp too. (Pause) And silence is 8. And between silence and sound is 7."
> *How was Ann's cough sounds and silence?*
> "Sounds and silence at the same time but not between."
> *If Ann talked at the same time would that be sound?*
> "Only politeness is sound."

She means "please," "you're welcome," "thank you," "excuse me"; for years she's been sensitive to these phrases, doesn't want to hear them, doesn't want to say them. *Hypersensitive.* And we don't know why. It's *Strange.* The categories bleed into each other, like watercolors on wet paper.

> *And ordinary talk?*
> "That is not sound. (Pause) And the bell in camp is a sound and also a silence, and a sound between silence."

The bleeding continues. The bell sounds three times, with intervals between — is that it? That bell was loud, but Jessy used to run upstairs from the soft click of the dishwasher, the low rumble when the thermostat tripped the furnace. Even today she covers her ears when she opens the refrigerator, in case the motor turns on. Auditory sensitivities are characteristic of autism. But the bacon-and-egg system, it's clear, includes more than sound.

"Doing something fairly bad is only 3 and bad is 2 and very bad is 1!"
What if there's a foghorn and *doing something bad?*
"That is 2. (Pause) Doing something bad is the most! No wonder get egg." (I begin to see; breakfast with only two pieces of bacon is incomplete and must be suitably supplemented.) "And you say a magic number is a sound too. And people scream out loud and shout and whistle is a sound too."
What is a magic number?
"8 is a magic number. 6, 4, 3, 5, 2, 1 is a magic number."
Not 7?
"And 7 too. (Pause) And all are, up to infinity. (Pause) If I have less than 6 and don't have any bread have a small egg or some of these fruit instead of egg. Egg is only for less than 4."

Now she goes into a graded system of substitutions for decreasing amounts of bacon. My mind is spinning, I don't catch it all. I revert to the numbers:

Are all the numbers equally magic or some more magic?
"1 to 8 is very magic. If I have less than 5 and egg I have to cut that thin slices of toast. If I have less than 5 and no egg I have to make thick slices of toast." And it goes on . . .

27

What envelope to put *that* in? A breakfast dialogue with a teenager; a plunge into the experience of autism.

It's all there, in that single conversation. Idiosyncratic Language. Hypersensitivities. Compulsions. Correlations. Numbers. But perhaps most important is the simple Social fact: at fifteen, after so many years of effort — ours, her teachers', her own — Jessy was really trying to communicate. Instead of ignoring my questions or fending them off with a convenient "I don't know," she was working hard to answer them. She had something she wanted to explain enough to propel her through the effort of putting words together. It was a matter of absorbing interest to her. She wanted to share it with another person. How normal, how ordinary — for an ordinary toddler, the toddler she never was.

And who but its creator could explain such a system? *Bad* — an emotional, perhaps even a moral category (but though normal toddlers continually say "bad cat," "bad mama," I realize now that I've never heard Jessy apply "bad" to a living being). Badness ordered into degrees, logically, numerically correlated to exact quantities of bacon, bread, fruit, to determine a breakfast menu. Strangeness suffusing the everyday.

.   .   .

There is no single entrance into the enveloping experience of autism. Jessy's strange systems, here glimpsed, require a chapter to themselves. I will not start with them, though more than anything else they reveal the way she thinks, its unique amalgam of simplicity and complex logic. Yet though language is not the core of Jessy's experience, it is only through language that her experience has — to some degree — become accessible to us. And it is only through language that our experience has become accessible to her — to some degree. So these opening chapters will focus on language, the gateway to a shared world.

. . .

I wrote the bacon-and-egg dialogue down as it happened, but it wasn't until afterward that I realized how much was hidden within it. Jessy's words had opened a window into the wordless long ago, lighting up what it was to be surrounded by sound, hearing it with preternatural sharpness, yet unable to give it human meaning. What counts as sound? As silence? *Ordinary talk is not sound.* Polite phrases are sounds — automatic, unchanging reflexes, almost meaningless. So are coughs and burps and bells and shouts and whistles. Jessy volunteered another example: "And animal noises just like a dog." (I remembered a midnight three years earlier, when Jessy screamed and screamed and wouldn't sleep because a dog was barking a mile away.) Jessy had defined meaningful speech out of existence. Talk all around her — we are a talkative family — understanding none of it; *sounds* for her were exactly what for us were mere noises. Sounds were simple, recognizable, intelligible, reliable, the same at every hearing. Only these penetrated Nirvana — emissaries, mostly unwelcome, out of the enveloping incomprehensibility. *And silence is 8. Because of good.* Silence makes no demands.

Certainly it was no longer like that on October 7, 1973. Now she was talking to me, understanding my questions, trying to answer them. But that was the way it had been. It was out of that bewilderment she had emerged. Emerged? Indeed. But her words themselves expressed how qualified was that emergence. Years had passed, years of daily effort, as her family, her teachers, and she herself concentrated on every means we could think of to enable and encourage speech. Five years before, her labored,

29

garbled words had been scarcely intelligible outside her own family. Now any patient listener might understand them. Yet again and again, to even the patient listener, the common words of our common tongue resisted common sense.

What was going on? Certainly Jessy's reality was not ours. Speech that communicated strangeness must inevitably be strange. But there was more to it than that. The ears that registered the softest, remotest click seemed unable to distinguish the essential sounds that make one word what it is and not another. The mind that grasped squares and square roots as if by instinct couldn't seem to get the hang of how her native language worked.

"I looked at the clock by mistake," she would say. Clearly it was important; Jessy would be shrieking, inconsolable by anything we could say or do. But "by mistake"? After years of bewilderment, one day it came to me: you can't *look at* something *by mistake*. Looking is a deliberate act. But you can *see* something *unexpectedly,* and we'd long known how distressed Jessy was by the unexpected. Could that be what she meant? It was possible. Spoken, heard, both words contained the same hard "k" sound. I began to pay closer attention to those agonized "by mistakes," testing my guess before I tried out what she thought of my translation, since it is all too easy to secure agreement from an autistic person who only partially comprehends your question and wishes you would go away. Jessy accepted the new word — more, over time it supplanted the bizarre original, to the point where one day she could exclaim, "I saw a star unexpectedly, I'm so sad!" She was twenty-five then, her vocabulary growing steadily in range and sophistication. Yet polysyllabic or seldom-heard words were still heard inaccurately and reproduced only approximately, as with a small child. Thirteen years later we would hear her remark, referring to something that might have happened but didn't,

"I said it ex post fracto." Surprised, we laughed. She laughed too, then added, "I didn't mean 'ex post fracto,' I meant 'hypothetical.'" A confusion of sound? Of meaning? The natural result of habitual inattention to a still largely unintelligible surround? All three?

I found out what Jessy was up against when we spent a season in France. I had thought I knew — Jessy was eleven and we had been working on language since she was two. But I had to become a foreigner to feel it. I had far more French than Jessy had English. Yet I was awash in a sea of sound. When people spoke directly to me — not from a distance, not as part of a general conversation — when they spoke slowly, distinctly, in words I knew, about a subject with which I was familiar, I could get the gist of what they were saying. An hour of this and I was exhausted. And this was what Jessy experienced every day. No wonder she tuned out, didn't, couldn't, pay attention.

. . .

I should make clear that though some degree of communication impairment is characteristic of autism, Jessy's speech is by no means typical. Most autistic people who do acquire useful speech eventually sound much like the rest of us. They may speak too loudly, or with less variation of tone, as might be expected of people who cannot gauge their effect on others, but their fluency, vocabulary, and syntax are generally on a level with their intelligence. I don't know another autistic person who functions as well as Jessy who has to labor so to assemble her words into something like English, who still speaks her native tongue like a foreign language. Dr. Wing, who saw Jessy at twelve, was struck by the gap between her nonverbal competencies and her speech; she concluded that her autism was complicated by another handicap,

31

aphasia, which affects the ability to acquire and use not only words but the syntactic structures, the deep grammar that is the armature of language. Though Jessy was five when she began to acquire a vocabulary of single words, it was years before she could put them together into a recognizable sentence. Even at fifteen it wasn't easy: "No wonder get egg." My account of Jessy's language in *The Siege* was written when she was eight. Knowing it would be the longest in the book I called it "Towards Speech: A Long, Slow Chapter." I couldn't know then that I had chosen the word "towards" not for her childhood, but for her whole life.

Much in that chapter still holds. I will not repeat it here; there is too much else to be told. Those with a particular interest in speech development may refer to those pages. Rather than linger on the details of that long, slow process — its steady achievements and its continuing limitations — I will let the anecdotes speak, those I've transcribed already and those to come. "A new fluffy-in-the-middle! Found in the newspaper!" What normal four-year-old wouldn't say "I found it"? "If I don't have any bread have a small egg." It wasn't the printer who dropped out "I will." Those who speak pidgin know it makes talking easier not to deal with the pronouns and auxiliary verbs, especially when your mind is struggling with what you're trying to say. "And people scream out loud and shout and whistle is a sound." The meaning is clear, but the grammar isn't. Jessy has all the foreigner's trouble with verbs and their transformations, with the indefinite and definite article, with pronouns of all sorts, with prepositions, with indirect discourse.

And simple, familiar words may come out even more oddly than "ex post fracto." Jessy was in her thirties when, in a thank-you letter for a birthday gift of sheets, she wrote, "I will wear them on my bed next week." Preoccupied with questions like

"What's next?" and "Who's next?" (she doesn't like them), one day she asked, "Is there such a thing as 'How's next'?" Another day: "You can say 'What are you looking for' and 'Who are you looking for.' Can you say 'Where are you looking for'?" When Hans Asperger spoke of the "original and delightful" language of his child patients, he was thinking of locutions like these. Jessy's speech difficulties may be intensified by aphasia. But I doubt that a person struggling with aphasia would ask such questions.

It is not only in such bizarre "originality" that autism and aphasia differ. The communication handicap in autism goes far beyond the production and interpretation of actual speech. Communication is a richly interactive process. Human beings communicate not only by words but by gesture, by posture, by facial expression, by "speaking looks" — by what we rightly call body language. Aphasia does not affect this kind of understanding; if an aphasic child is thirsty it will use hand and mouth to mime drinking from a cup. The autistic child will not do this. Nor will she look at you or make an interrogative sound. Rather, she will take your wrist and lead you to the refrigerator. Unable to read the silent indicators with which human beings communicate as surely and significantly as they do in words, Jessy was adrift in a far deeper sea. The following chapter will tell some of the linguistic instruments that have helped her navigate.

CHAPTER 3

"When the time comes"

January 1989. More than a decade ago. We're going away for a few days; a friend will be looking in on the cat. Jessy tells him, "I will teach you to feed Daisy when the time comes." I compliment her; I have long ago internalized the principles of reinforcement. "How nicely you said that."

"I learned that from you," she says. Then, "What does that mean, 'when the time comes'?"

I try explaining, give up, tell her she really knows because she said it right. And she does know, because right away she supplies her own paraphrase. "In the future," she says. With that to go on, I can elaborate: the time is indefinite, yet it will come. Five minutes later (she's been worrying that we'll run out of garlic, though we have several cloves) she remarks, "I will buy garlic when the time comes." Of such small triumphs is progress made. And seeing me writing down our exchange she notes: "You will file that under Verbal" — as of course I will.

. . .

What would we do without these conventional phrases? We'd do fine, we're told; the studied avoidance of such convenient formulas — clichés — has become a hallmark of good writing, speaking, thinking. But for her they are not merely what they are for us, easy shortcuts to familiar meanings. Spend time with Jessy — years and years, say — and you can see how they serve not only to ease speech but to organize experience, to identify it, to articulate its recurrent patterns; how they enable her to cope with it, even, to some degree, to understand it. "I learned that from you."

Jessy returns to these clichés again and again. She likes them, she *uses* them. So anxious over uncertainty, indefiniteness, anything that escapes strict predictability, she welcomes, *needs,* this prefabricated language. It helps her pattern the inevitable fluidity of being in the world. Once it was patterns of action that steadied her, routines that she tried to keep as invariant as possible. She still has these, but now there are also patterns of words. We can't be sure when we will go shopping, when we will leave for the summer, when a friend will arrive. "I will hang loose." A kitchen knife is missing. "Things come and go." It doesn't erase the anxiety, but it can assuage it. And to someone obsessively concerned about small mistakes, it's comforting to hear that there's such a thing as a "margin of error." If naming perfectionism can't control it, it can at least bring it to consciousness, where it can be worked on. "No big deal." "Nobody's perfect." She can repeat the words, though she's still far from accepting the fact.

Perfectionists do not make mistakes. They do not forget things. Jessy will wail, "Oh, I forgot to" — add the salt, empty the trash — though her "forgetting" has lasted less than a minute. Eventually I thought of a mollifying trick of language. "Don't say you forgot, say you almost forgot." And today, after the usual "I forgot," she herself, her voice now audibly relaxed, supplies the paraphrase that is the guarantee of understanding. She even puts a positive spin on it: "I just remembered."

Phrases can express her relief: something happened "in the nick of time." They can modify her impatience: "one step at a time." They can structure the weather, though like so much else, the weather may resist; Jessy complained that the "January thaw" was late this year. Language has power, not only to grasp but to order. This year Jessy picked up "downside," applying it to overtime at work, distressing because it tends to be unexpected. It's become second nature to reinforce a new idea. "Yes," I say without thinking, "everything has a downside." But *Jessy* is thinking. "And a compensation?" I know how she got there; she's generalized from our previous discussions (oh, so many!) of overtime, its compensation, of course, a bigger paycheck. Downside, compensation. How right, how proper that there should be this pair, maintaining the world in benign and orderly balance.

When her bird was mopey, her parakeet book supplied the needed reassurance, a chart of symptoms, serious and not so serious. Jessy loves charts; they too reduce an untidy world to order. The parakeet's condition became identifiable, placed under a heading I wouldn't have thought of; it was, it seemed, a Passing Indisposition. This has become an invaluable household concept, especially in the cold season.

Do these phrases also help her cope with the frustration of being unable to communicate? That's plausible. But it's surprising how little we see of such frustration. Jessy's frustrated when she tries unsuccessfully to do things. But in talking? She seems unconscious of the effort her speaking costs her. Nor does she seem aware of any inadequacy in her language. She knows she took a long time to learn to talk; we've told her that. She has even suggested some "good reasons for not talking," among them "being a baby" and "being a dog." But being able to talk, or talk better, is not one of her concerns. Although she dislikes intensely the gentlest suggestion regarding her behavior — she'll respond with a furious "Why do you correct me?" — she doesn't mind, she may even laugh, when we correct a tense or suggest she rethink her choice of pronoun. Her clichés help her express herself, but their real advantage is far more fundamental. They help her give structure to chaos.

Does that sound a bit too existential? Perhaps it wouldn't if we could remember what it was to live amid unintelligibility. But though we were all babies once, it wasn't for long. For Jessy that unintelligibility has lasted and lasted. How much even now does she understand? She needs the reassurance of words that can order her world. For years she could do no more than scream at its stubborn deviations. Screams might, though in the absence of language they mostly did not, reestablish the routines that structured the surrounding flux. Kanner's primary marker of autism was an overwhelming desire for the preservation of sameness. That was Jessy's desire — that Nirvana should remain inviolate, an island safe from change. She knows now that this is impossible. But words are available now, preassembled, replicable, reliable. Like maps, like charts, like calendars, like schedules, all of which she read easily before she could read texts, they allow her to lay hold of her experience, bring it under the mind's control.

But they can do more than that. By their very conventionality they can enable her to relate her experience to the experience of others. "That the way it goes," she'll say. Be reassured: there are patterns in experience. There are word patterns to correspond. By them Jessy begins to navigate, not only in space and time ("Things out of place bother me," she says), but in the mysterious world of human beings.

. . .

"When I work late I say to myself, 'An ounce of prevention is worth a pound of cure.'" It comes from Jessy so naturally it startles me. Certainly she's heard me say it. Though I don't much like clichés, I do like proverbs — reservoirs of social experience, rich encapsulations of generations of social wisdom, too easily forgotten these days, wisdom and words together. But in this case the applicability of this proverb isn't obvious. Testing her, I ask: "What's the prevention? What's the cure?" And she answers that working late prevents the backup of work in the mailroom. She has not only understood the proverb, she has generalized it to a new situation. Better yet, she is consciously using it to control her overtime anxiety. Of course I write it down. But should it go under Social or Verbal?

Social behavior and speech are linked inextricably. Jessy got interested in proverbs in her midtwenties, when she began to reach out for more ways of understanding the world. Literal-minded like all autistic people, she began to pay close attention to these figurative expressions. "A stitch in time saves nine" made literal sense when she was mending her sweater; it was easy to stretch it to cover other household repairs. Other proverbs were more metaphorical, yet she wrestled them into meaning, recognizing in them the ordering power of language. Proverbs are reassuring for someone who worries obsessively whether the weather will be fair or where my glasses are. More for my satisfaction than hers, I quoted my grandmother to her: "Sufficient unto the day is the evil thereof." I didn't expect her to listen, but she heard it, all right: "Day is sufficient until evil come out." It had surpassed her verbal powers but not her comprehension, for she not only explained it as "Don't worry too soon," but herself supplied the equivalent "Don't borrow trouble" and "Don't cross the bridge until you come to it." She had to work with that one: "Does it mean go over that bridge or go under?" But she got the meaning; when the cat was gone all day ("Lost, oh lost!") and came back at midnight: "Unnecessary sadness! And there wasn't any bridge!" Three months later, the weatherman predicted sunshine but clouds threatened. Jessy began to obsess, then checked herself. "It would be crossing the bridge too early — I would fall in the water."

They are useful, these idioms; they have become idioms because they speak to the human condition. No use crying over spilt milk. Getting off on the wrong foot. Getting up on the wrong side of the bed. So, of the dinner invitation I almost forgot: "If you forgot, then remembered in the middle of the night, then you would get out of the wrong side of the bed in the morning." Yet the application isn't always easy. "Tracy got out of the wrong side of the bed because her father was in a bad accident." *You don't say that.* Verbal patterns help, but they can't cure.

Still, they help a lot. Waiting is very difficult for Jessy, whether it is for a month or a minute. Is it because predictability, the trustworthiness of the environment, is threatened? Is it because Jessy, so accurate with clocks and calendars, can't gauge her experience of subjective time? I don't know, but waiting, at work or at home, is a continual problem. All the more welcome, then, what Jessy's made of my grandmother's "All things come to him who waits." They mostly do, and Jessy crows exultantly her own version: "Things come to me when I wait!" It makes it, I think, *and Jessy thinks,* just a little easier to wait next time.

.   .   .

Jessy is not only reassured by these linguistic patterns, she enjoys them. I don't think it's a coincidence that it was in the same years

39

she began to use proverbs that she made her first verbal jokes. She has grown up in a joking household; that, I think, has made her less solemn than most of the autistic adults I've met. I remember her father, long before she could talk, laying her down on the kitchen floor, saying "Night-night," covering her with a newspaper and giving her some kitchen object to hold as her talisman blanket, teaching her to enjoy the discrepancy between reality and pretend. We thought then that we were teaching the actual difference between the two, but I know now it was the enjoyment that mattered. Even as a tiny child, Jessy never confused the imaginary and the real. Like most autistic people, she operates in the realm of the visible, the tangible, the literally true. What we were teaching was that perceiving the difference between what was true and what wasn't could be *fun*. I treasure the memory of *her* first joke, when she lugged over a snow toy, a "flying saucer" almost as big as she was, offered it to a guest as an ashtray, and *laughed*.

Still, it took many, many more years before Jessy was at home enough in language to make a joke in words. At first it was hard to tell if they were really jokes, as when, seeing me about to sneeze, she said she'd read, not my mind (we'd talked about that) but my nose. But we laughed, and she did too, clearly enjoying the unexpected thing she'd done with words. Word play became more frequent. Though our cat's name was Daisy, we often called her "Kitty dear," and Jessy echoed us. One day she saw a daisy in a field and addressed it as "Kitty dear." A simple (mis)association of ideas? A pre-pun? She laughed, at any rate, and that made it a joke. She was ready for puns; she learned the word at once. "Two days ago I saw somebody cut hair in the mailroom — 'just a hair.' That is a *pun!*" And it was; she'd remembered her father's way of saying "just a little bit."

The pun, I was told as a child, is the lowest form of humor, and hers are very simple. "Cold pills is pills that are out in the cold!" "The microbus is the bus with microbes in it!" But this one shows real observation. "Eclipse Rum" — the label caught her eye, at a time when she resonated to anything about eclipses. "Eclipse can eclipse the pain and eclipse the insomnia. That is a pun."

Indeed, and more than a pun. It is a step beyond the literal, into further, richer dimensions of language. No giant step, however; Jessy doesn't take giant steps. Twelve years have passed since then. Eclipses have lost their fascination; these days it's anything to do with Merrill Lynch. So we read from the morning paper: the company is downsizing. "A certain number of people are going to be cut." *"Cut?!!"* The astonishment in her voice makes it plain: the autistic literalism survives. They are to be mastered one by one, the slippery ways of words.

Some, however, she will not master. After forty years we know that. I need to say more about Jessy's difficulty with pronouns — a difficulty which, though it may seem too specific to be of general significance, points far beyond itself to some of the most important areas of current research, into the psychological and biological nature of autism.

. . .

Among the autistic characteristics that Leo Kanner noted in the brilliantly observed paper in which he first identified the autistic syndrome was "pronominal reversal." He based his report on eleven cases; along with literal and stereotyped language, he noted pronominal reversal in eight of them — and the other three had no language at all.

> There is no difficulty with plurals and tenses. But the absence of spontaneous sentence formation and the echolalia type of reproduction [have] . . . given rise to a peculiar

41

grammatical phenomenon. *Personal pronouns are repeated just as heard* [emphasis his], with no change to suit the altered situation. The child, once told by his mother, "Now I will give you your milk," expresses the desire for milk in exactly the same words. Consequently he comes to speak of himself as "you," and of the person addressed as "I.". . . There is a set, not-to-be-changed phrase for every specific occasion.[1]

Just so; autistic speech begins as echo. When Jessy at last began to request things, that's what we'd hear: "You want a cookie?" She was six. She was eight when I finished the first long, slow chapter on her speech, and she still did not refer to herself as "I." By then, however, she echoed the word — and reversed the meaning. "I" was her mother. That, after all, was what she heard me say.

Since then there has been great progress. Her sentences are longer and more complex. They are fairly correct grammatically. They reach beyond herself to other people. Yet even so, these are the kinds of things that may come out when she has to deal with pronouns:

"I think I will eat with us," she says. "I" is securely in place, but "us" is an uneasy surrogate for the plural "you" that should denote me and her father. Even the "I" may get lost: "You wrote you a check." Who did? It was she who had paid me for her share of the groceries. "We will have to borrow our car." It was the neighbor who needed our car. Two pronouns at the same time are just too hard to handle. She speaks of Miranda, her brother's daughter, and someone asks, "Who's Miranda?" She hesitates. Then, slowly and carefully, she replies: "I . . . am . . . my niece."

Be assured, Jessy knows she isn't her niece. Although eager psychoanalysts for years took pronominal reversal as evidence of "early ego failure," Jessy has anything but a weak ego. Still, they were right in suspecting that something more significant was going on than peculiar grammar, more pervasive than a mix-up of two pronouns. Yet however tempting "I" and "you" might be to ego psychologists, they are only the tip of the iceberg. Jessy has even more trouble with "we" and "our" and "us," with "they" and "their," with "his" and "hers," even with "he" and "she." I hear her answering the phone, groping for the words to tell a caller her father's not home. It's going slowly, so I try to help. "Say he's not home and can you take a message." Jessy alters the primary pronoun; she's learned that much. But what results is this: "She's not home, and can you take a message."

So what *is* going on? "The pronominal fixation," wrote Kanner, "remains until about the sixth year of life, when the child gradually learns to speak of himself in the first person, and the person addressed in the second person."[2] At six, when Kanner's children had sorted out their pronouns and had "no difficulty with plurals and tenses," Jessy's difficulties were just beginning. Obviously, their speech handicap was less severe than hers. *Because* it was less severe, Kanner could think of pronominal reversal as an isolated — and temporary — grammatical oddity. And because he noticed no difficulties in plurals and tenses, he could not see how closely all these — and other — characteristics of autistic speech are related, or the deeper problems they point to.

Consider these examples, all from Jessy's third decade. "I better remind Daddy about my dental appointment." "We are having chicken livers for dinner." "My supervisor said I'm going away for Christmas." The first two seem to be perfectly ordinary statements, and the third, though a little odd, is at least possible. Except that it wasn't Jessy's appointment, it was her father's. Except that she'd already had dinner; she wasn't included in that "we." Except that it was the supervisor, not Jessy, who was going away. Jessy knew all these things; she is the last person to be confused about matters of fact. It was the words, the slippery, shifting words, she couldn't handle.

Kanner had it right. She couldn't change the pronoun "to suit the altered situation," least of all when she had to manage two pronouns and correctly relate them to each other. Pronouns shift. Nouns stay still. She had no trouble with "Miranda," as she had spoken her own name years before she referred to herself as "I."

The altered situation: that's the key. And what has altered the situation? Its external constituents are unchanged: the dental appointment, the chicken livers, the vacation, even the people referred to. What has changed is the interior situation, the *point of view*. Point of view is what determines the choice of pronoun. *His* appointment. *You* — you two — are having chicken livers. *She's* going away. Pronouns must be adjusted, changed from first to second or third person, from singular to plural, often both at the same time. It's complicated even to write about; how do little children manage to learn to do it?

Recent research suggests that they do it, easily and naturally, because they have a "theory of mind." Never mind the grandeur of the phrase; consider instead the implications of the experiment Uta Frith and her colleagues reported in 1985. The situation is simple: an experimenter, a child, and two puppets, Sally and Anne. While the child watches, the puppets act out a little drama. Dr. Frith describes it: "Sally has a basket, Anne has a box. Sally puts a marble into her basket. Sally goes out for a walk. While Sally is out of the room, Anne (naughty Anne!) takes the marble from the basket and puts it into her own box. Now it is time for Sally to come back. Sally wants to play with her marble." Now the investigator is ready to ask the key questions: "Where will Sally think her marble is? Where will she look?"[3]

Obvious, isn't it? A normal four-year-old will get it right: Sally will think it's in her basket, because that's where she left it. It's equally obvious to an autistic child. Sally will look in the box. Why? Because that's where the marble *is;* he saw Anne put it there. He doesn't consider what Sally thinks. He doesn't *know* what she thinks. Autistic children, writes Frith, "have no problems in understanding what it means to see and not to see something . . . but they cannot understand . . . somebody else's attitude or belief."[4] They have no "theory of mind" — of what goes on in other minds. Without that, how can they make sense of how people speak of others, how they speak of themselves? A normal two-year-old may reverse "I" and "you." But it isn't long before he works it out spontaneously. He hears his mother say "I" and realizes she means herself; soon he reflects that realization in his own speech. He's recognized two perspectives, hers and his own, and adjusts accordingly. He doesn't need to *echo* pronouns; he *understands* them.

Of course if a child cannot recognize attitudes and beliefs, the effects reach far beyond language — beyond mere grammar or fluency into all the interactions, spoken or unspoken, between human beings. Frith's subsequent research confirms what parents know and autistic adults themselves report: that even if speech at length develops normally, even if I.Q. tests as superior, the difficulty in perspective-taking remains. That social handicap is at the core of autism, and it will occupy the fourth part of this book.

Pronouns are only a few of the words whose choice depends on our perspective, the view from where we stand. "Here" for you is "there" for me; "ask" for you is "tell" for me. Jessy reverses these too. In "I am my niece," it isn't only the pronoun that is skewed. "She *is*": the verb must shift with the person. There are all sorts of words that give Jessy trouble. Consider "some" and "any," and their paired but very different meanings. When Jessy remarks, as she did one day at lunch, "Sometimes people don't like to do anything," it sounds like an observation on the human tendency to laziness. Still, I'm puzzled; this remark seems to have no relation to what we've been talking about. But when she adds that "people are different" I understand. Change "anything" to "something" and it comes clear. Jessy wanted Dad to balance our checkbook right away, and he said he didn't feel like it. (People are indeed different; Jessy loves to balance her checkbook.) The problem is long-standing; I recall the eight-year-old who converted "somebody" and "nobody" to "one-body" and "zero-body," trying vainly to pin down what is indefinite by its very nature.

Such peculiarities are only partly explained by a difficulty in perspective-taking. They point us to another core characteristic of autism: to that "anxiously obsessive desire for the maintenance of sameness" which Kanner noted in 1943.[5] Change happens, of course; it can't be avoided — not outside Nirvana. But tell that to the child who's shrieking because the bus has taken an alternative route to school, or because a random act has disrupted a pattern only she could see. It can't be avoided in the world, and it can't be avoided in that reflection of the world that is human language. From the beginning of its slow development, Jessy's language was pointing us to the cognitive disability hidden in those emotional reactions. She wanted the world to stay still, *needed* it to stay still, because if it would only stay still she could understand it.

The children relate better to objects than people. Kanner noticed that too. *Objects don't change.* People do; their expressions, their voices, their every word. Jessy understood objects. When she was still speechless and uncomprehending, she stacked blocks, put rings on a stick, sorted shapes and colors. At three, she surprised the psychologist who tested her by rapidly fitting twelve different shapes into a form-board. He concluded she had no mental deficiency. And she didn't — not in the realm of the unchanging, the absolute, the thing that is what it is. (I've written at length about this in *The Siege,* so I'll be brief here.) It was *relative* concepts — and the words that express them — that divided what she could learn easily from what she couldn't master. As I wrote in that earlier book, "What she was able to grasp were absolute terms . . . — those that reflected concepts that could be . . . understood in themselves. 'Box,' 'cat,' 'giraffe.' 'Rectangle,' 'number,' 'letter.' What she could not understand were relational terms — those that must absorb their full meaning from the situations in which they occur" (page 204).

A giraffe is a giraffe wherever you find it; a rectangle is a rectangle. Not so with nouns like "teacher," "friend," "sister." My teacher may be your sister, or her friend. It was not until late in Jessy's teens that we could teach her, with charts and written examples, the simple words for generational relationships. Or are they simple? Now, at forty, she can say Miranda is her niece, getting the noun right if not the verb or pronoun. She knows she herself is Miranda's aunt and my daughter. If I asked her, I think she could tell me that her sisters are also Miranda's aunts, that her brother is Miranda's father, that her mother is Miranda's grandmother and her niece is my granddaughter. Even now, though, I'm not sure she could manage more than one of these shifting relationships in the same sentence.

Certainly this too is a matter of perspective-taking, of "theory of mind." (House for you is home for me.) But we must ask a further question: *Why* is it so hard for autistic children — and adults — to assume another's point of view? In Jessy's childhood I was content to think vaguely of a "social instinct" that normal

47

children had and Jessy lacked. At that time there had been little research into the way these children's minds actually worked; Sally and Anne were far in the future. There had been even less interest in the brain pathology that might underlie autistic characteristics — not surprising when psychiatric opinion was generally satisfied that autism resulted from damage done to a previously normal child unlucky enough to have a refrigerator mother.

In the past twenty years, however, biological research has taken off. In 2000 alone the National Alliance for Autism Research, founded (by two parents) only five years earlier, was able to fund sixteen new projects. Many others are sponsored by universities, medical schools, and the National Institutes of Mental Health. (Informed and useful summaries of promising work may be found in *NAARRATIVE,* the alliance's quarterly newsletter. See Appendix III.) They lead in many different directions — into the mechanisms of information processing, the possibility of a mutated gene, the role of serotonin in brain development. Particularly significant in understanding what might explain that missing "social instinct" is the work of Eric Courchesne, professor of neuroscience at the medical school of the University of California at San Diego.

Courchesne's research allows us to make sense of so much that we've observed in Jessy: her problems with pronouns, with relational language, with perspective-taking, with *people,* with everything that requires her to respond flexibly and rapidly to change. His hypothesis — and through magnetic resonance imaging he has amassed hard evidence for it — is that damage to particular locations in a baby's cerebellum reduces the capacity to shift attention from one sensory stimulus to another. Consider an experiment in which the subject must disengage his attention from a visual cue — a red flash — and shift it to an auditory cue — a high tone. *Autistic children take up to ten times longer to do this than normal, or even retarded, controls.* Even high-functioning adults take three times longer. Like the Sally-Anne test, the experiment sounds simple. But its implications are equally profound.

Imagine, says Courchesne,

> a child focusing on a toy airplane he holds in his hands. Mother comes into the room and the sound of her foot-steps captures his attention. He turns and listens closely as she suggests reading a favorite storybook while pointing to the shelf where it is kept. At the mention of the storybook, he shifts his attention from his mother's words and gesture to his bookshelf, where he scans his array of books, look-ing for his favorite. When he spots it, he points to it, and he yells, "There it is!" and shifts his attention back to his mother, awaiting her response.

How ordinary. The average child can do something like this at eighteen months. How ordinary — and how complicated.

> Four things have happened in the attentional and sensory world of this child. First, the child is stimulated by sensory information that he must process. Second, despite focusing his attention elsewhere, salient changes in auditory stimu-lation, mother's footsteps, were detected, alerting the child to potentially important information outside his immedi-ate focus and capturing his attention. Third, after redirect-ing his attention to mother's words and actions, he maintains attention, listening closely and watching care-fully for specific, important information. Fourth, when he

sees and hears that specific information, the name of his favorite storybook and the gesture pointing to the shelf, he acts on that information by shifting his attention to the visual stimuli across the room. Again he focuses his attention, this time on a colorful array of books of various sizes, looking closely at each one for the specific book he now has in mind. When he detects it, he shifts his attention back to his mother.[6]

And if he can't do all this, rapidly, easily, naturally?
You have an autistic child. You have Jessy.

. . .

Who at eighteen months was snaking a chain up and down, up and down, for twenty minutes, half an hour, longer. . . . Who at forty, focused on the Weather Channel, hears nothing I say. Who sees me get up to answer the phone yet informs me it's ringing. Whose biggest problem at work is her unwillingness to interrupt one task and switch to another. She isn't ignoring me. She isn't inattentive. She isn't contrary. She's doing the best she can with the cerebellum she was born with.

No wonder she responds late, or not at all. No wonder she perseverates; it's *hard* for her to disengage her attention. No wonder she leaves out verbs and articles and pronouns and prepositions, in what those who know autism call "telegraphic speech." No wonder she likes proverbs and clichés, language that is repetitive, predictable, formulaic. No wonder she likes *experience* that is formulaic. When she watches TV, what is she watching for? Not the content, whatever that may be; not even the pictures. What she's listening for, what she *hears,* is what we've named "in-transition phrases": "Coming up next," "Don't touch that dial,"

With characteristic concentration, Jessy checks the accuracy of her painting against a photographed detail.

Jessy at work in the Williams College mailroom.

left: Making salad as her brother watches. In the background, some of Jessy's greeting cards.

below: Mother and daughter talking together ...and reading together.

above: Hanging out the wash. Note the muscular tension in hand and arm. Jessy does nothing by halves.

right: Jessy and her father spot something in the sky.

Sister, brother, and three summer housemates celebrate Jessy's birthday.

In the midst of family picture-taking, Jessy "snaps," so suddenly that father, mother, sister, brother, and brother-in-law are still smiling. Jessy likes this picture.

Happy and at ease in the T-shirt her brother gave her, Jessy displays the phases of the moon.

"Hold everything," "Stay tuned," "Be right back." She is delighted to write them down for me. She has identified twenty-six.

. . .

Jessy is doing the best she can, and she's doing pretty well. People who knew her twenty years ago are amazed at how her speech has improved. That didn't just happen — it has been the result of hard work, hers and ours. It has become second nature to speak to her directly, in words within her comprehension. It has become second nature to ask, not tell, so she must try to answer in her own words. It has become second nature to ask only what we judge she can answer. If we judge wrong and she seems at a loss, it has become second nature to fall back to an easier question, prompting her toward the goal she can't reach unaided. It has become second nature to teach what normally needs no teaching.

Of course I would rather not teach Jessy language. To impose forms of language is to impose forms of thought. Better she should "pick up" words, ideas, spontaneously, naturally. But Jessy could not absorb language out of the air. I watch four-year-old Miranda playing with the telephone, dialing it, talking into it, the rise and fall of her voice mimicking her mother's. Her play is practice. She will not have to be taught, as Jessy was, to identify herself by name or rehearsed through the shifting pronouns of "He's not here, may I take a message." But that was years ago. Though autistic children become autistic adults, they do get better at listening and attending. Jessy now is picking up, yes, picking up for herself, phrases she can apply in much more complex situations. That is one of the slow, infinitesimal miracles that carry us forward.

Last month I went to the Stop and Shop without my discount card. I knew my lapse would become a subject of conversation;

Jessy is intolerant of other people's forgetting as well as her own, and she is particularly interested in supermarket cards. She scrutinized the sales slip; she determined that the card would have saved two dollars and forty-five cents. She talked about it, talked about it, talked some more . . . And then, to my surprise, she disposed of it with a relaxed "Oh well, it's only money." I never taught her that! But it's there and will be there again (and again) — when the time comes.

CHAPTER 4   "Guess what!"

T hat was another long, slow chapter. This one will be shorter, since it deals not so much with what Jessy says, or the words in which she says it, but with something harder to convey: how she *sounds*. We encounter people through their voices. Sound shades into meaning: all sorts of messages reach us through these tones that can express everything from desolation to ecstasy. They too are aspects of Jessy's language, deeply, intimately part of who she is.

You don't have to hear Jessy say more than a few words to know that you're not talking to a normal person. Quite apart from her stereotypic phrases or her telegraphic speech or the strangeness of what she may say, she sounds *different*. The difference is familiar to everyone who works with autistic children. Lorna Wing speaks of their "monotonous or peculiar vocal intonation"; developmental psychologist Bryna Siegel notes their "atypical tone of voice," "flat, atonal," "unmodulated," "consistently 'off' in some way"; an atypical *prosody,* to use the technical term,[1] prosody that like Jessy's may continue into adulthood.

Face to face, over the phone, at a distance, Jessy's voice is instantly recognizable. Though her repertoire of tones is characteristically limited, it is very much her own. "Guess what! 70003 is a prime!" Already exclamation points pepper these pages, typography's pale attempt to capture the confident, positive voice in which Jessy, who was once thought to suffer from "early ego failure," announces her discovery. "Guess what! Every galaxy has lots of sun families! Know why I say that? Pretend the sun is the parent and the planets are the children and the earth is *me!*"

Those examples are from years ago, relics of outworn enthusiasms, but "Guess what!" is still Jessy's trademark. More often these days it registers not actual discovery (and certainly not a genuine invitation to guess), but something subtler — a kind of satisfaction in assertion, in factuality, definiteness, in something noticed, verbalized, properly pinned down: the fee in feet. It's the happiest of what we've come to call her openers, the start-up phrases she uses, needs, to propel her into the enterprise of speech. Some of these are brief and commonplace: a protracted "well . . . ," perhaps, a "but" or "and." Listen, however, and you realize they don't work like other people's ands and buts. "And" doesn't announce an addition; "but" doesn't introduce a qualification or contrast. "Because," a very frequent opener, heralds no assertion of causality, though Jessy understands cause and effect very well. It's just another word from the start-up grab bag, establishing a holding pattern while she gets together what she will say next, reminding us, as we wait for the words to come, of the brain-based difficulty she experiences in shifting from one stage of speech to the next.

Other openers, more elaborate, share some of the enthusiasm of "Guess what!" "I can't believe it!" she'll say, or "Isn't it amazing?!" That's not a question, though it sounds like one, and it's

not really amazing, even to her. Rather it's her regular introduction to a matter of consuming interest — a new fluffy-in-
the-middle, perhaps, or a fee. Yet the exclamatory tone may communicate only the mildest of surprises: "But couldn't believe it,
they decided to make the fireworks [originally scheduled for
eight] at nine!"

She doesn't need openers for the routine exchanges of daily
life; if you're shopping with her, or working with her in the
kitchen, she'll sound almost normal. "Tomorrow I am going to
make Doubly Delicious chocolate cookies" carries no exclamation point. On such familiar ground, she offers with no hesitation
an ordinary, factual communication. There are plenty of these
now; it's more than thirty years since I noted down that for the
first time in her life Jessy had told me something I didn't already
know. But other statements sound more normal than they are. I
hear Jessy say clearly, definitely, positively, "Jane's house is in
New Jersey." It *sounds* like a statement, it's a statement in tone
and form. Yet she doesn't know where Jane's house is, and the
statement is false. But she has no reason to mislead me, and she is
incapable of a convincing lie, so I'm able to guess: this is one of
her odd assertions that function as a question. What we do auto-
matically is for her an effort: to shift the verb and noun from
"Jane's house is . . ." to "Is Jane's house . . . ?"; to turn a statement
into a question. Jessy knows how to do it; she can do it in writing,
taking her time. But in speaking she'll go for the easier way.

.   .   .

Jessy asks surprisingly few questions; that particular rising tone is
rare. She never went through a "why?" stage; even "when?" and
"where?" are not among her common openers. When apparent
statements function as questions, they are not the questions of

55

curiosity; they are not even requests for information. The assertion is in fact a hopeful hypothesis; it is that particular kind of question that expects a "yes" answer. "Jane's house is in New Jersey, isn't it?" She'd like it to be there; she has reasons for wanting to go to New Jersey. But instead of dealing with that (it's a long way), I opt for a speech lesson. "Is that a statement or a question? Are you asking me or telling me?" I've taken a risk, I know. This time she answers calmly, and we talk about other ways she might say it. But sometimes — beware — the lesson hits a nerve. She may bang the table, she may explode into what she and we call a snap. "Why do you ask me that?" It's more than a nasty, sharp response. And it's not a question; it expects no reply. It's a *sound,* loud, abrupt, angry, immediate, no openers necessary. The words come out so fast they are scarcely recognizable. This is not communicative speech, it's a reflex noise. Though we've learned the kind of thing that elicits these snaps, that doesn't mean we understand them. They send us back where we started, into bewilderment.

Other expressions of emotion, however, are only too easy to read. Suppose Jessy is asked, as she often is at work, to interrupt one task and turn to another. She's learned what she should say and she says it: "I would be *happy* to." The tone is not flat; on "happy" it rises high. Too high; the exaggerated emphasis proclaims she wouldn't be happy to at all. The disconnect between words and feeling is complete. It's the sound of insincerity; give it a bit of a twist and it might even be irony. Yet it is neither. Insincerity and irony are beyond Jessy's powers; for her, language means only what it says. She has learned what is required by the situation, she has said the right words; what more can be expected? Without a theory of other minds, one is unlikely to interrogate one's own; Jessy doesn't consider whether she really is happy, or realize her voice conveys not happiness but clear displeasure.

Yet Jessy has a genuinely willing response, a cheerful, relaxed "Sure." I praise it whenever I hear it, and I hear it often. But at work, where it's most needed? Shall I coach her, rehearse her to substitute the simple answer that comes out so naturally when feeling is congruent to word? It won't work. I know already the unnatural grin that results when she's asked to smile for a photo. If she tries to mimic the tone, her voice will betray her more reliably than any polygraph.

And shall I try to explain insincerity, that inherent denial of literal meaning? I could tell her, "It's when you say something but you don't really mean it." She'd understand that, I think. But that doesn't mean she could say a good "Sure."

.   .   .

She can't lie. That's almost true. Ten years ago it *was* true. Today, now and then, she manages the transparent lie of a three-year-old caught with his hand in the cookie jar; she's come that far. I'm not the only parent of an autistic child to count it as progress. Real lying, however, controlled, effective insincerity, is forever beyond her compass.

The inability to lie convincingly could pass as a diagnostic indicator of autism. It's not surprising that it's mirrored by a corresponding inability to recognize dissembling and deception; both, after all, depend on a developed theory of mind. Temple Grandin, an established professional, speaks of her difficulty in allowing for the possibility of insincerity; Paul McDonnell, a college student, tells us how easily a "friend" was able to borrow, then to steal, the money he had worked all summer to earn.[2] Temple and Paul navigate in the world as Jessy cannot, but they are like her in this. Autistic people are no better at recognizing insincerity than performing it.

The lies Paul's friend told him are what Jessy calls "black lies," to distinguish them from the white lies that I have reluctantly taught her are sometimes necessary — polite lies, social lies, lies to spare people's feelings, lies to smooth the way, saying you're happy to when you're not. I can feed her the words; the tone is beyond my control — and hers. How well, after all, does she understand the tones behind our words, the irritation in my voice, the controlled exasperation when her supervisor finds her once again doing something she's been told not to do? Paul McDonnell writes of how "certain tones of voice" made him anxious, when he would "think that a surprised tone, or an emphatic tone, would mean anger" and ask his parents, "Are you mad at me?" over and over again. Without the understanding of tones — and gestures, and facial expressions, even postures — how can one be sure? Can one even distinguish black lies from white?

.   .   .

There is a dimension of language, however, that Jessy does not share with Paul and Temple. No account of Jessy's language would be complete without her noises, not only those loud snaps, but a whole array of other sounds, private, unconscious. Higher-functioning autistic people may have made such sounds as children, but they learn to keep them private, as they learn by experience to restrict body motions like rocking to places where they will not attract attention. Jessy has learned too; after twenty years these noises are seldom — I hope never — heard at work. At home, though, they are so much a part of her that we scarcely hear them, unless in the increasingly rare instances when they escalate and she needs our help to regain control. More often, however, they are simply noises. I overhear her squealing as she vacuums, not anxiously, not cheerfully — just squealing. Absorbed in the activity and in the privacy of its covering noise, she is hurrying to finish before she leaves for work. She's left herself plenty of time, so her squeal is unworried — unlike the squeal, similar but edged, that I hear through the sound of the shower when somebody opens a tap and her water turns cold. Or the "Oh dear," irritated rather than distressed, amid a softer squeal punctuated by just enough words so that I gather she's dropped one of my morning pills and it's rolled under the stove. No big deal. All is quiet again; I know she's found it.

And there are, or were, the mumbles, dark, ominous, existing in a no-man's-land between verbalization and pure sound, as involuntary as her furious snaps. The snaps, at least, are interpretable; though "Why do you ask me that?" expects no answer, I can hear the meaning beneath: "I'm really angry when you ask that kind of question." But the mumbles were subverbal, idiosyncratic word clusters devolved with repetition into nonsense, nonsense that was nevertheless a reliable indicator of discomfort or displeasure. The mumbles flourished all through her teens. She and a perceptive friend spent hours once happily listing them, twenty or thirty utterances, each more bizarre than the last. "Cigar three, cigar three," was one. Years later, her articulateness and communicativeness growing together, she explained how that began: it was "she got a three" — a strikeout. So today I ask her about another one, equally mysterious: "*We* go on." I'm putting some mumbles in the book about her, I tell her. Where did that one come from? She's delighted to remember; she always is when we summon up remembrance of things past. It was from a Led Zeppelin song, she says. Another, "Dig a roof," from a song she sang at camp. "Root?" I suggest, searching, as usual, for

59

meaning. No, she says, "roof." If I knew the song, perhaps . . . I can guess it was, like a third strike, associated with something unpleasant, but I'll never know how or why.

She reminds me of another mumble. We heard it often — back then we heard them all often. It sounded like "anklyeah." She's clear: there were no words hidden in that one. Rather, it represented the number seven. Leaving that oddity, I hazard another question: "You don't mumble at work, do you?" I've phrased it to invite the answer I want to hear, I know. Still, I'm delighted by the cheerful force of her reply. "No way!"

Because there can't be mumbles. There mustn't be. I remember the middle-aged woman I encountered in a bus station, mumbling under her breath to nobody at all — the frisson I felt, of pity but also fear. Jessy was still young; my imagination leapt ahead. Would she be like that, grown too old to be charming, still mumbling? If I felt fear, what could I expect from others? Higher-functioning people can learn from experience the necessity to control bizarre behavior — experience unlikely to be pleasant. Jessy needs explicit teaching. "You don't want people to think you're crazy, do you?" I didn't even know then if she knew what "crazy" meant. Enough that she knew it was bad, that it included mumbles, and that if she tried hard she might learn to control them. And over years, she did.

Today, however, she is enjoying herself. She volunteers a mumble I've never heard her say, noting, with her usual precision, that it is "out loud, which is not really mumbling." It's out of the same bag of mysteries, though: "You caught my name." "Call?" I ask — her pronunciation is ambiguous and I know she hates us to call her name. But she's definite; the word is "caught." "Keep me from crying," she adds. "Crying makes my face all stuffy." I'm pleased. I'm proud. At forty, she's developing her own method of control. If it works, who cares that it's bizarre? For "crying" means the banshee wail, of all Jessy's sounds the climactic worst. "*Wee*-alo, *Wee*-alo" it goes, up and down, up and down, in an ecstasy of desolation. It's rare now, and brief, but still the same syllables, the same piercing, tuneless tune: our own domestic air-raid siren.

In the weeks spent writing this chapter, listening more closely than ever before, I've heard sounds I never noticed — within the squeal, for instance, the occasional squeak when Jessy's task requires an extra application of force. How much else have I not registered? Her prosody is more complex than I thought. Experience must qualify those opening adjectives; her communications are not so much flat or atonal as unvarying; the impression of monotony is less a matter of unchanging tone as of tone that changes always in the same way. Tone and phrase are one package, inseparable. "*Here's* the local forecast." It's high on "Here's," to catch our attention, then drops almost an octave. The prosody is as stereotyped as the language, as stereotyped as the situation (breakfast means we watch, *must* watch, the Weather Channel). "*Mo*ther." She's brought my tea. That's routine too, but to her mind less urgent; the tone drop is less marked, more like a major second. Her bedtime "Good night" is relaxed, almost musical; up on "Good," on "night" it descends to rest.

Every utterance has its own tune. "Ups-a-daisy doo doo doo!" marks annoyance. The voice waves up and down on "Ups-a-daisy," flattens out on the "doo's." This exclamation point transcribes emphasis, not the confident enthusiasm of "Guess what!" What happened? No big deal; she's cooking, and "the bacon didn't flip over." A less transitory irritation yields something stranger, its tone blending annoyance with resignation: "Oh well, hang hang!" Then there's "Oh I'm so sad!" There's emphasis, but her voice is calm. She's a *little* sad, but it's under control. Another expression of sadness isn't really an expression; it's more like a claim. "Oh *no!*" This is Jessy's regular response to disaster — earthquake, hurricane, train wreck, death. It may be in Canada or China; certainly it involves no one we know. Nevertheless, touchingly, Jessy will reach for the appropriate verbal package. Yes, it sounds fake. But it's the best she can do.

Though disasters are common, oh no's are relatively rare. Mostly they are elicited by newspaper stories, or conversation only partially understood. Jessy's around during the TV news, but she pays no attention to the screen's vivid horrors. They cannot pierce Nirvana. Yes, she may express irritation or sadness, she may experience the transitory desolation of wee-alo's. But her language is who she is; I must insist on the primacy of that shining "Guess what!"

Yet this week I heard something even better. I heard her say, "Come see!" Common words, ordinary sounds, nothing bizarre about them. Words I had to wait forty years for. Come see. Share this experience with me. Together we will look at something with joint attention. It doesn't matter what. I'll write it down. And we will share the exclamation point.

PART TWO

Thinking

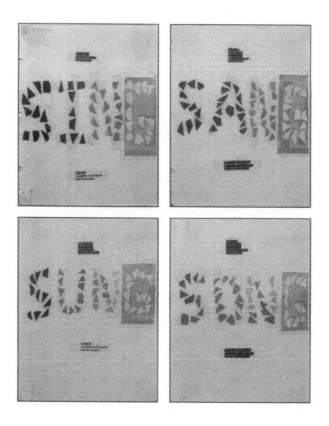

CHAPTER 5   "All different kind of days"

Scraps of paper are enough now, and a kitchen folder. In those days, though, the house was full of paper — notebook paper, construction paper, and more and more computer paper, the old 11-by-14 sheets, lined or faintly striped, brought home by her father for a child who drew so much more easily than she talked. There was still little speech in those days; my language notes are largely from Jessy's last twenty years. It was paper that allowed us to glimpse her mental experience, that assured us that though she might not talk, might not understand, she thought.

The records of her thinking fill not a folder but a heavy suitcase, and they are far from complete. Many disappeared at once into the whirlpool of a busy household. Some she cut up into the tiny squares we called her "silly business," to be sifted up and down, up and down, between her fingers. Still, opening that suitcase now, exploring it anew, trying anew to comprehend it, I am overwhelmed by the sheer volume of its contents. Alone, often by choice, sometimes by necessity (for however we worked to breach her isolation, someone could not always be with her), year after

65

year she drew, she painted, she penciled her scraggly capitals and numbers, applying the simple skills we'd taught her to the materials we provided. I would come home, find new sheets, save them or lose them. It didn't matter. Next day there would be others.

The suitcase records the critical years of Jessy's growth — roughly from age nine to sixteen. Revisiting it, exploring it not a sheet at a time but in its full accumulation, I am overwhelmed by more than volume. To write the past is to discover it. I am overwhelmed by the expenditure of mental energy it represents, by the sheer *activity* of a mind that in its inaccessibility could seem so empty. At three, wordless, Jessy had lined up objects in rows and we had thought that must, *must* be a sign of intelligence. Now we could see intelligence's paper trail. The pages that follow are an attempt to unpack the contents of that suitcase.

. . .

Imagine finding this on a piece of paper:

NO
KNOW
YES
KYESW

It's logical, isn't it? It figures. It is no weak or torpid mind that spontaneously processes KNOW into KYESW. It is a mind that has searched for a rule and found it. Language doesn't work by logic, but Jessy at eleven wasn't interested in language. She was passionately interested in logic, in principles that could introduce order into a world still largely incomprehensible. The purest logic, the surest, is the logic of number; Jessy's numbers came from the same period. They have their own box, almost as big as the suitcase; I'll unpack it — some of it — in the next chapter.

The suitcase drawings too displayed numbers — everything was connected in that busy mind. But the pictures and letters moved beyond the abstract numbers and shapes that had formed her early kingdom, into a world rooted, however strangely, in her daily life, a world recognizably human.

Even KNOW and KYESW impinged on meaning; Jessy, perforce, had long understood NO, and (though it took more teaching) YES. She was using letters more and more. Even three years earlier she had written MAMA, and formed — logically — the plural MEME on the model of MAN and MEN. I was delighted with KNOW and KYESW, as I was delighted with every sign of intelligence, but I didn't think much about it at the time. Later I recognized it for what it was: a written record, one of the first, of the systematic quality of Jessy's mind.

To systematize is to discover regularities and organize them. Like MAMA/MEME, this system was still very simple. Jessy's interests then were focused on numbers, systematizable in so many more ways. A few years later, however, numbers were receding in favor of words. She was fifteen. She talked more, and more clearly. She was beginning to read and write. And what more significant to write than her own name? JESSIE, JESSY, JESS, JES, JESSE, JESSICA.

Here is what Jessy told me on October 21, 1973. It is no coincidence, I think, that it's from the same year, even the same month, as the bacon dialogue; that was the year she began to respond to questions with more than yes and no. (It would be many years more before she could offer an explanation on her own.) Since the questions are obvious, I record only her answers:

JESSIE. Because of sunny. And sometimes I say -ICA with a sunny.
And cloudy is JESSY.

67

And JESS is bad.
And very bad with only one S — JES.
And -E is between good and bad — JESSE.
And with -ICA is a good day. If I in special day sposed to
write this one — JESSICA.

What makes a day bad?, I asked. "All because of cry and mumble
and bump is a very bad."

.   .   .

Yes, it figures. It figures even better than I realized. Only now, as I
write, do I discover the system within the system, how the number of letters decreases, a letter at a time, from six to three, from
sunny goodness to very bad, then increases to the full affirmation
of the seven-letter special day.

It all connects. It does more than connect, it correlates. (Jessy
learned that difficult word instantly; as with "heptagon," she
already had the concept.) Bacon, egg, toast, badness, goodness,
sound, silence. The brilliance of the sun. More precisely, the
number of its rays, twenty-four for a really good day, sixteen for
good, twelve for average, grading down to one, even, alas, to zero.
Jessy generated systems as naturally as she breathed. They proliferated spontaneously, without outside reinforcement; the bacon
system had been going on for months before we noticed it. More
than anything that happened at school, systems were what exercised her intellectual and emotional energy. Although her engage-
ments with the world were so limited — *because* they were so
limited — she could bestow on her systems a singlemindedness
unavailable to a normally diversified experience.

A mother is not the most graceful witness to her child's intelligence. Fortunately there are others. Jessy was twenty-three, the
bacon system long past, when two psychologists, Lola Bogyo and

Ronald Ellis, became fascinated by the range of what Jessy could (and could not) do. They studied her for months. They gave her every kind of test. It isn't easy to test an autistic person with limited speech and comprehension, particularly when she is intolerant of errors. With extraordinary sensitivity and imagination, Lola and Ron found ways to make the testing process fun, so that Jessy loved her weekly sessions. Here is how they describe her "fascination for the creation and elaboration of systems."

> It became clear that at the root of these systems lay a remarkable ability to induce the rules and regularities that characterized any set of items — numbers, words, objects, or events. [Jessy] not only induced these rules, she systematically and obsessively explored all of their possible applications. From numbers, colors, and common objects she created complex, intricately ordered systems, some of which she used, it seemed, to structure her world, and some of which she merely played with, endlessly delighted by their order.[1]

To explore the limits of Jessy's "inferential skills," the investigators tried a test expressly designed "to measure an individual's aptitude for abstraction and rule induction." They chose the Raven's Progressive Matrices, a nonverbal test suited to her "agrammatical" speech and a comprehension "impaired for complex messages." I cannot better their description:

> This test . . . contains a series of problems graded in difficulty. . . . Each problem consists of a pattern or matrix from which a piece is missing; the subject is given a set of alternatives and must choose the piece that completes the whole. Simple problems consist of a homogeneous pattern

(e.g., a grid of dots) from which a piece has been "cut out." More difficult problems present patterns consisting of disparate elements related by subtle and complex rules; simultaneous variations on several different dimensions (e.g., shape, size, orientation) must be attended to in order to induce the underlying regularities.[2]

Normal subjects start fast and slow way down; Jessy "quickly began to turn the pages, pausing only to glance briefly at the patterns and point immediately at the missing piece. We waited for her to slow down and falter. We waited in vain." She scored "well above the 95th percentile for 'normal' adult subjects." Her friends shifted to the Advanced Progressive Matrices. "Again we watched with amazement as [Jessy] turned the pages more quickly than we could consider the choices. Once again she scored above the 95th percentile, this time being compared to graduate technical and medical students."

Given [Jessy's] limited language skills, we wondered whether she actually knew and could articulate governing patterns or whether she had somehow been able to guess which pieces would make the wholes "look right." . . . Despite her stilted broken sentences, she was unfailingly able to name the relevant dimensions and features, to articulate the rules governing their progressive alterations, and to describe how an extrapolation of those rules generated the correct pattern. It was clear that to [Jessy] these rules and regularities were obvious, self-evident in the designs themselves. She seemed puzzled that the solutions needed any explanations at all — as if we had asked her what shaped peg would fit best in a round hole.[3]

It was there. The vigorous intelligence her siblings were putting into exploring history, learning Tibetan, writing novels, and negotiating their lives, in Jessy was streaming into this one channel.

. . .

Jessy reached everywhere for systems in those days. Together we looked at a Tintin book; Tintin, lost in the desert, sends a message. But what she took from the story was not adventure but a system. Tintin sent us to the encyclopedia; days later I found a sheet on which she had, accurately and without book, written out the full Morse code. I started her on the piano; I was surprised, though I shouldn't have been, at how fast she learned musical notation. But these experiences, meant to enrich, remained void of content. Jessy had no interest in tapping out a message, and though she had an excellent ear, she took no pleasure in making music. Systems were enjoyed for their formal qualities, not their use. Someone gave her a junior-high dictionary, each word briefly defined and illustrated by a simple sentence, perfect for a beginning reader. She spent hours poring over it, and we rejoiced. But what was she doing? Searching out regularities, discovering the few that English can offer. She thought about them, talked about them, wrote them down. Elf, elves; self, selves; shelf, shelves; half, halves; calf, calves; knife, knives; wife, wives; hoof, hooves; leaf, leaves; sheaf, sheaves . . . "How about 'reef, reeves'?" she asked. "How about 'roof, rooves'?" The dictionary was crammed with meanings, gateways to knowledge and communication. We watched as Jessy, surrounded by words, now at last hearing them, seeing them, even reading them, drained them of meaning, to be absorbed into her world of abstract formalisms.

Language, of course, resists abstraction; if it didn't we'd all be speaking Esperanto. Jessy picked up a ski resort's chart of weather conditions. Cold, Very Cold, Extreme Cold, Bitter Cold; a snowy universe reduced to four categories. Unfettered by meaning, Jessy could extrapolate, and did. *Her* chart read Good, Very Good, Extreme Good — and Bitter Good.

Maps, like charts, are formalisms. Jessy mapped her neighborhood, she mapped our journey route by route, all the way from western Massachusetts to Rhode Island. She diagrammed floor plans of familiar buildings. Systems ordered space; they ordered time as well. Jessy liked printed schedules, calendars, clocks. Telling time was so easy for her that we wondered the more at the effort it took to nudge her through familiar words about familiar subjects. Reading was hard; it demanded more than an ability — even a preternatural ability — to discriminate patterns of letters. It insisted on meaning, and meaning offered Jessy no rewards. But what joyous energy she poured into locating "sheaf" and "sheaves"!

. . .

Shortly after her fourteenth birthday, Jessy made a book. There was nothing remarkable about that; following on our early work with picture communication, Jessy had been making picture books for years — rapid scrawls, uncolored, reflecting TV cartoons, children's stories, and the rituals of her own daily life. This, however, was not a picture book. It contained neither drawings nor sequential narrative. Rather, it was a celebration of the transformations of a word.

The book was a thing of beauty, a theme and variations, four words in three colors: SING, SANG, SUNG, and SONG (see page 63). It was also a finely organized system. It was not, however, as remote from daily life as it appeared. Jessy had an additional source of inspiration — a bag of cookies. How she must have scrutinized it, alone in her room, to note the possibilities of its three shades of coral, its corresponding greens, its contrasting white! Never mind crayons; here, in this bag, were her materials. Patiently she snipped the colors into bits, 208 in all. Each word had its own page, the three-inch letters formed of the snips, SING and SANG in coral, a different shade for each letter, SUNG and SONG in green to correspond. Except for the four final G's; for these she had reserved the white snips, backing them with coral and green cutouts so they would show up on the white pages. Nor had she forgotten the cookies; they were part of the pleasure. Neatly she cut out their labels, Assorted, Cashew, Almond Crescent, Chocolate Chip; these too became part of the ensemble. Still she was not done. Logic propelled her forward; to the fifth page she taped swatches of her base colors; to the sixth, finely balanced collages in all six shades of coral and green. The seventh page she had reserved for a larger, climactic collage in — what else? — white on white.

The whole was strangely modern, even postmodern, except that Jessy had no idea of what such terms might mean. When I asked her, on a hunch, "What is the name of that art?" she didn't say "Collage," as I thought she might. Her answer was both specific and accurate: "Those are the cookie art."

·   ·   ·

I can describe the cookie art, as I can describe much else that we did together or that Jessy later told me about. But the system of systems, the supersystem that in those days eclipsed every other, reflected and conditioned the whole of her emotional experience, encompassed everything she most cared about — that is not mine to describe. I learned about it second-hand. It is time to pay tribute, however inadequately, to the many others who shared

73

devotedly, year after year, the enterprise of helping Jessy grow. I long ago lost count of them; besides the members of her own family there have been more than fifty. It wasn't I who taught her to tie her shoes. It wasn't I who taught her to ride a bicycle, to knit, to weave, to draw. And it wasn't I who worked out the organizing principles of Jessy's supreme, her most complex, creation. An eighteen-year-old mathematics student at Williams College figured it out, helped in the write-up by Jessy's father, and it is right that work I did not and could not do should be told in their voices. So I quote, and at length, from David Park and Philip Youderian's article "Light and Number: Ordering Principles in the World of an Autistic Child." Imagine, then, Jessy as she was at thirteen:

> [Jessy] listens to hard rock with an expression of the purest joy, rocking in her rocking chair, putting her hands over her ears when it is too much to bear, for this is the music of o clouds and 4 doors.... No clouds at all, the sky the radiant image of a pleasure so intense that to bring it down to a really bearable level would, she shows us, require 4 closed doors between her and the phonograph. It is, she explains, "too good," but she can bear it for a while. The music changes; the rapture abates by one degree: 1 cloud, 3 doors. The classics, most of them, rate 2 clouds and 2 doors; *andante espressivo* brings protests, 3 clouds and 1 door; and worst of all is a spoken record, 4 and o. The sum of clouds and doors is always 4, and ... even the sun loses some of its rays when the music is not of the best.
>
> [Jessy] always watches the phases of the moon and knows where it is in its cycle. On the nights following a

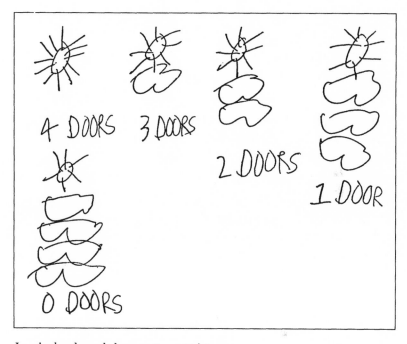

Jessy's clouds-and-doors system, spring 1970.

full moon, it rises outside [her] window and stays for several hours partly visible behind a large tree. Behind [her] door there is intense excitement, the sound of running feet and little cries of joy. [Jessy] is looking at it — she will not say its name but refers to "something behind the tree" — running from window to window to see the light travel behind the branches and the shadows creep across the grass. The shadow cast by a house standing in the light of the full moon is the most exciting and beautiful sight in the world, and in these long evenings everything depends on there being no clouds to spoil the pleasure. If the moon is obscured, [Jessy] lies in bed and cries her tearless autistic cry. The moon is the number 7, and so is the sun, and so, apparently, is a cloudless sky.

. . . When [Jessy] sets the table for dinner, she puts a tall glass by her plate. It is green, her preferred color, and it is divided into 8 equal levels by decorative ridges. Into this she pours her juice. It too is green. On most days she will fill the glass exactly to the sixth or seventh level. Sometimes it will be filled to the top; occasionally it will be lower. Ordinarily, the exact level is determined by the type of day with respect to weather and the phase of the moon. "All different kind of days," depending on sun and moon and weather, are the heart of her system.

The system contains 29 kinds of days. . . . The two most important factors that govern the category of day are the position of the sun in the sky and the presence or absence of clouds. . . . [A day with zero clouds is what Jessy calls *dayhigh* (in summer when the sun is high) or *daynothing* (in fall, winter, and spring). These] are the best of all, celebrated by a full glass of juice. The level of juice is twice the number of doors, down to the disastrous *daybump*, when [Jessy] has been a bad girl. . . .

[Jessy's] mood depends on the sky. During *dayhigh*, and even more during *daynothing*, she is cheerful, joking, and cooperative. Clouds, especially if they come to spoil *daynothing*, bring despondency . . . , and clouds covering a full moon are the worst of all.

Most *daythings* [Jessy's word] have numbers, in which the digits 1, 3, and 7 predominate. Most of the numbers are primes: 7 is good, 3 is bad, but almost always 3 is associated with 7. The numbers 73 and 137 are . . . magic, and the concept of days in general belongs to their product $73 \times 137 = 10001$.[4]

And so on, for ten pages, two tables of correlated phenomena, and a page and a half of intricate calculations. The splendors of the system defy summary; even the investigators didn't understand them all. Those who share a fascination with numbers can explore them further in what they wrote.

But whether or not we could follow the numbers, we all had to live with the system. It was a rich and inclusive *we*. No one person, or family, could provide all that Jessy needed to grow. There was always someone else working with her in those days. Most of these Jessy-friends lived with us, some for a summer, some for a year or more, Jessy's therapists, teachers, and good companions. They were college students, most of them, though two of the best were still in high school. None had any training in special education or developmental psychology, but I claim for them the word "therapist" without hesitation. They worked with Jessy, played with her, sang with her, joked with her, comforted her, understood her secret words, interpreted her to strangers, devotedly taught her whatever they could. Endlessly inventive, endlessly generous, without them hers would be a different and sadder story.

Some, like the young mathematician, recorded their observations. Most did not. But one, it seemed, kept a journal, and after more than twenty-five years, knowing I was again writing about Jessy, she sent it to me. Its entries remind me of what I had gladly forgotten; they bring back how very hard it was, for Jessy and for the inclusive *us,* in the days when the system ruled. Fran came to us when Phil had moved on. It is her turn to speak.[5]

Pure blue sky. *While walking the long hill, a little cloud appeared and covered the sun briefly — oh, what sadness and anger — mumble mumble, looking down at the ground, dragging the feet, stopping, answering no more questions about school.* "What is the matter, Jessy?" "The cloud over the sun." *I told her, after the cloud was no longer over the sun and was now just in the sky, that she only needed to be a tiny bit sad, because the cloud was small and the blue sky was big. No help, mumble mumble. Finally the cloud went behind the mountain and trees. "Jessy, the cloud has gone away." Jessy was happy again immediately.*

The cloud, it turned out, was "full of numbers," multiples and powers of 37 and 73, with two bad 3's. Jessy drew it in a picture, with herself and Fran, when the cloud was gone and it was all over. But the weather was not always so obliging. "Some days are almost all bad," Fran wrote a month later. "Full Moon. Low, heavy clouds. What a horrendous day." Jessy came home crying; someone had taken her special seat on the school bus. (There was a system there too, but we never understood it.) She refused to sing with Fran ("I will cry again") or answer her questions. She mumbled because the radiator hissed. She cried when she made a mistake in sewing, stopped, cried some more. When Fran tried to comfort her she went in her room and told Fran to go away.

I walked out the door and cried all the way home. It was just too much of a struggle all afternoon. . . . I cried and cried, as bad as Jessy, I suppose. . . . No work Tuesday. Hooray! A holiday for a full week. I must rest, and be renewed to begin again.

There were good days too, with swimming lessons, walks, bicycle rides in benign weather. With Fran's encouragement and supervision, Jessy designed and sewed a gorgeous quilt, the sun on one side, the full moon on the other, not a cloud in either sky. And the system kept on growing, spreading invisibly, underground. As it predated its discovery by others ("Found these at years and years," she told her father), it evolved without their attention. What Fran had glimpsed would prove to be its next and most florid stage.

Moon, sun, and clouds were now correlated with, of all things, flavors. And gum wrappers — twenty-nine of them. Fran didn't know it, and I didn't notice it, but of course that was the number of *daythings,* real and imaginary. There were also (only now do I discover it) twenty-nine of the numbers in the pictured cloud. So it was *not* good when three wrappers were missing. "No remedy. Mumble mumble and threats of tears." But this time Jessy found a way to cope. She drew the number-filled cloud again and cut it into tiny bits to sift between her fingers. "She played with them all afternoon. A Decent Day."

Jessy told Fran there was a new kind of cloud, "rice rice pudding with lime rice pudding."

Jessy had made tubes of many flavors with numbers on them, which were the same as the [numbers on the] cloud. . . . She started to make a chart of suns with the same flavors (lime lime lime, little bit lime, rice pudding, etc.). She wanted me to go away, but I had her tell me about school first, and then she continued to make the flavored suns, neatly in rows.

Then she cut them out. Those suns are in the suitcase, twenty-nine of them, their rays recalling the emotional valences of days past. Jessy drew them short and stubby, so as to allow room to do full justice to the colors of the coordinated flavors. Rice pudding, for example (not good — correlated with 3), had to be drawn in grain by grain, a painstaking operation, since Jessy classified the grains as "fairly big," "big," and "extra large." The flavor tubes are in the suitcase too, in a twenty-nine-, then a forty-one-tube

Flavor tubes (detail), another of Jessy's systems.

version. Jessy taped six sheets of paper together so she could draw them all. From each tube emerges a length of icing. "This is a happy frosting come out the tube," she explained. "And sometimes sad."

The lengths are carefully measured to correlate with the appropriate number. Each digit, Jessy told me later, equals one inch, each exponent (squares, cubes, et cetera) a half-inch. Three, the smallest number, occurs twice; the inch-long lengths of icing are labeled "rice pudding with lime." The largest number is one even a mathematician would find bizarre:

80

$$7^{2\infty^{\infty+1}} \times 37^{2\infty^{\infty+1}}$$

(Seven squared to the infinity power to the infinity power plus 1, times 37 squared to the infinity power to the infinity power plus 1.) It is represented by a 9½-inch length; its icing equivalent, carefully written on the tube, is "lemonlemonlemonlime little tiny bit orangeorangeorangelemon." The composition of the 8½-inch length is even more complicated: "double dutch little bit lemon-lemonlemonlemonlemonlimelimelimelimelimelimelimelime-limelimelime." And Jessy colored the icing as carefully as she calculated the numbers, in permutations and combinations that boggle the mind. The next tube is identical except that "little bit" becomes "little tiny bit"; predictably, the little lemonlime-green areas that stripe the brown chocolate have been reduced by half to correspond. I could describe the others, but somehow I don't think I will.

The correlations came first. The explanations emerged only gradually, as her language grew more adequate to what she had in her head. We learned that flavors correlated with the times she "looked at the clock by mistake." They correlated with the number of times she soaped herself in the bath, 0 light blueberry, 1 lime, 2 lemon, 3 orange, 4 strawberry, 5 vanilla, 6 licorice, 7 chocolate, 8 grape, 9 or more, blueberry again. "Dark lemon," "dark lime," and "lime with a little bit rice" correlated with three kinds of "striped" cloud. Even her pencil line proclaimed the system. "Why is the window all wiggly?" I asked of a drawing showing Jessy in bed and the moon behind her favorite tree. It was because of the flavors, she said, wiggly for lime, three-eighths wiggle for lemonlime, whole wiggle for rice pudding. How many other correlations were there that we missed?

The system expanded to include new experience. A year later, when the Christmas catalogs came, the various delicacies received numbers, 137 for solid chocolate, 173 for chocolate with nuts, 337 for chocolate with coconut. Dobosh torte was 3; with cherries it was $7^{\infty+1}$. That same number, she told her father, was correlated with airplane vapor trails: if two vapor trails crossed, the cloud at the crossing point yielded $7^{2\infty+2}$. The exponential 7 was "rice pudding with limelime"; a 3 was rainbow-colored "when cloud has color outside looks like rainbow and white inside." In the system's last stage Jessy correlated colors, flavors, and numbers with her typing errors, and correlated *them* with "flavor cookies." A surreal connection? It proved to be wholly logical when Jessy drew herself with ten cookies, two on the floor. "And drop the cookies. That is a mistake." So both kinds of error were duly recorded in a Book About the Mistakes, in which the very word was given its permutations: "mistakable, mistake, mistaken, mistaker, mistakers, mistaking, mistook."

Then, gradually, numbers lost their magic. Three years later she could say, "They used to be important to me, about all the things, such as bath soaps, and wild berries, and too good music and crying silently and laughing silently." We heard no more about flavor tubes. Jessy's emotions seemed independent of the weather. She stopped making books. She was doing more conventional art at school, and told us, echoing, I'm sure, what she'd been told, that she was now "too mature." For all we knew, the system was finished.

And yet, twenty years later, when we got out the tubes and suns and "all different kind of days" to show Dr. Oliver Sacks, it turned out it was still there. Under his gentle questioning it burgeoned anew. There had, she said, been more than twenty-nine days; Phil just hadn't had room for them all. She named and described them. She added fifty-five new flavors, including dark rum, three kinds of "expresso," and tangerine. "There are *lots* of correlated!" she crowed, reaching the end of the list.

. . .

If the reader by now is experiencing some wandering of attention, that's as it should be. For us normals, boredom is part of the experience of autism. We are, most of us, impatient with formal structures we cannot relate to the concerns of human life, and even mathematicians, who are sympathetic to such pure pleasures, expect them to lead to something more interesting than tireless and self-absorbed variations on the same theme. We taught Jessy to solve simple equations. Excited by her facility with numbers, Phil tried to teach her calculus. But she resisted, not because she couldn't understand it, but because it had nothing to offer her and demanded much. Rather than repeating familiar processes, it insisted she move forward, beyond the security of the predictable into a realm in which she must accept, even invite, unexpected results. And that was exactly what Jessy did not want. Her systems were designed to eliminate the unexpected, to capture uncertainties in a net of connections, to reduce them to rule.

Marvelous yet sterile, they bespoke a mind which for all its vigor was severely limited. Kanner's "preservation of sameness," Courchesne's "difficulty in shifting attention," worked in tandem to restrict both the ability and the desire to initiate new activities. Chaining, lining up objects, sifting silly business — these had been the preferred pastimes of Jessy's childhood. In adolescence she could still be content with repetitive activity, rocking in her rocking chair, bouncing her superball up and down (though she might use her new skills to graph the number of bounces). At least her systems were richer experientially than that. They could admit new elements — weather, typing lessons, words and their spellings. Some were pleasurable; many were not. Systems couldn't banish the world's distressing variability, but they could set it in order, as clouds, cookies, mistakes, and shining days and nights took their places, subjected to the mind's control.

. . .

But Jessy's in her forties now. Understanding most of what is said to her, much of what is said around her, much of what is *done* around her, she has much more to occupy her mind. She can think about her bank statements, about the estimated tax forms necessitated by her new Roth account, about what she'll make for the upcoming potluck supper, about when to renew the permit for the landfill, about whether it's time yet to order a new bag of basmati rice. I could make the list much longer, but I won't; normal activities can seem pretty boring too. Yet Jessy doesn't find them boring. She is as absorbed in noting them, remembering them, keeping track of them, as she once was in her systems. She finds her regularities now in the humdrum exigencies of the world around her. She is our authority on the schedule of public holidays, the rules governing the acceptability of donated blood, the times the bank and post office open and close. Collecting information, storing it, using it, communicating it, her mind is at work. That is enough. The bizarre glories of the system have faded, as glories so often do, into the light of common day. But we are content. The common day is the day we hold in common, the day we can share. "Come see!"

CHAPTER 6   "When I ten, *that*
minus one!"

It wasn't the most gracious way for an eleven-year-old girl to welcome the neighbors' new baby, but it certainly showed a grasp of number. Jessy's formulation provided yet another illustration of the social blindness that is at the core of autism. But just as arresting as her substitution of a numerical relation for a human one, or her use of the impersonal "that" to refer to a living, breathing baby, was the unexpected sophistication of her spontaneous subtraction. "Genius" is in general an overused word, never more so than in its casual application to autistic achievement. Jessy's "minus one" was as accurate as it was inappropriate. But though it astonished, it didn't come out of nowhere. Before squares, before primes, before 37's and 73's and 337's, there had been years of the ordinary, grade school applications of number, as we worked to prepare her for what we hoped would be some sort of education beyond what we could give her at home. In fact we were preparing her, though we didn't know it, for the calculations that would make possible the System. So I must briefly leave the teenage Jessy and trace the progress of that preparation.

Jessy at a number-filled blackboard.

In its early stages, when Jessy was eight, numbers didn't seem particularly interesting for her or for us. They were something she could do, that was all, and with a child who did so little, that was enough. So there we were, she and I, day after day, down on the floor, crayons at the ready. I'm a bit bored, more than a bit; I'm drawing row after row, sheet after sheet, of triangles for her to count then color, the inspiration the Halloween corn candies that like other candies were such an important part of her small universe. There was no pressure; there didn't need to be. Jessy liked repetition, she liked counting, she liked counting some more. She liked coloring with her mother, both of us fixed on this simple, unchallenging activity. She liked it when I added another triangle and showed her the plus sign. I was teaching notation, not ideas; I knew that. But unawares I was also teaching something more important. Shared attention! The phrase, and the research behind it, was far in the future. But here we were, together on the floor. Another day, another sheet.

Jessy had been in nursery school four years when the nice teachers had to tell me they couldn't keep her among the little ones any longer. After months of corn candies, she could do more than keep track of missing washcloths, she could add and subtract on paper. Her numbers were scrawly and her 5's turned backwards, but her answers were right. So when September came I took her, wordless and unresponsive, to the principal of our local elementary school and showed him her numbers. He didn't bother with politeness — he thought they were all done by rote and said so. He didn't have to explain the subtext: an intellectual mother pushing an incapable child beyond what she could possibly accomplish. Jessy lasted only eight weeks in the special class. There was no "right to education" for the handicapped in those days.[1]

87

But to push Jessy beyond where she was ready to go was not what the intellectual mother could do, even if she had wanted to. Words must come before numbers, I thought, as they do in life — in normally developing life. I need not hurry my daughter into what came naturally. So we moved into multiplication and division slowly. Another year. More sheets. Corn candies were succeeded by the heart-candies of Valentine's Day, the kind that carry a word or two like LOVE or KISS ME, so we could also work toward words. More rows: times tables, 1's and 2's and 3's, then more rapidly (it was all so easy) up to 10, as the operations in her head were made visible, then assumed their conventional written form: +, −, ×, ÷. So why not fractions? I remembered how hard they'd been for me, but I was not Jessy. Hearts turned to circles, to rows and rows of pie charts, ever more complex. So why not one step further, letters for numbers, the beginnings of algebra? Jessy might not know the right way to talk about a baby, but she had no problem with that. It was as obvious to her that $a + a = 2a$, $a \times a = a^2$, $a - a = 0$, as that $1 + 1 = 2$. As for -1, wasn't it equally obvious that that was what you'd have if you took 1 away from zero? So there it was, all in place: "When I ten, *that* minus one!"

. . .

It's not surprising that so many autistic people are more at home with numbers than babies. Mathematics too is a language, but a language that is predictable, logical, rule-governed, blessedly abstracted from shifting social contexts. Teaching Jessy the ways of numbers was like providing a natural athlete with a ball and bat. Whereas words . . . I wrote words on the candies — NUT, CUT, HUT (a lesson in phonics), common words, her own name — and Jessy would reluctantly read them. But then she'd veer away, transforming them into nonsense: JESSY, JASSY,

88

JISSY, JKSSY, KESS. (Still, she'd inferred the rule. "Throw away N," she told me. "Can't say NUT. Just say UT, yes!")

We kept on with candies and circles till Jessy was past eleven. She was used to them, and I wanted to ensure that the abstract operations stayed meaningful, anchored in things that could actually be counted. But it became clear Jessy no longer needed them, if indeed she ever had. As with the washcloths, she had no trouble with real-life calculations. When she was nine, late in 1967, it occurred to me to ask her, "How old will you be in 1975?" It took her less than three seconds to answer, "Seventeen." Numbers had become more than an acceptable pastime; she grew enthusiastic as two-digit multiplication and long division opened up new possibilities. "Multiply?" she'd ask. "Fractions?" After two years of pie charts she summed up her progress, proudly remembering, "When a little girl, can't reduce to lowest terms!"

Numbers, good in the abstract, expressed the world. And they expressed *her*. As her twelfth birthday approached, we saw some very unusual numbers: 11 351/365, 11 71/73, 11 359/365. What could they mean? Then we understood; with characteristic exactitude, Jessy was calculating her age. Two weeks short of her birthday: 365 − 14 = 351 days. One week short: 359 days. And ten days? 71/73? That's what you get when you reduce 355/365 to lowest terms!

Age eleven was when Jessy took off on her own. Now she made her own sheets; she no longer needed a mathematical companion, though a resourceful helper taught her to calculate areas. Megan drew diagrams and Jessy solved the problems handily; she understood their connection to the real world. But the world that was most real to her was not that of our everyday bread-and-butter problems. With the necessary notations and operations in place, numbers, not words, became Jessy's primary expressive instrument.

We can't know how great a part circumstances played in Jessy's annus mirabilis. For we were not at home in her familiar house full of built-in activities; as once before, when she was four, her father was on sabbatical. We were living ten floors up in a small apartment outside Paris. No toys — not that Jessy played with toys much — nothing but paper, pencils, and a typewriter. In the cold, cloudy spring, only the activities we could think up. Prodigiously inventive, Megan lured Jessy into reading, typing questions to which Jessy typed out answers in a progressive dialogue. She typed out, in *words,* all the numbers from 1 to 100; it turned out she could spell better than we knew. The typewriter was good for numbers; with Megan she converted fractions to percents and solved simple equations. But Jessy could not be constantly accompanied. Alone in her own world she pursued different calculations.

Clocks became fascinating when she learned that the French numbered time not in twelve hours but in twenty-four. She drew a ten-hour clock, a twelve-hour clock, a fourteen-hour clock, sixteen-, eighteen-, twenty-four-, and thirty-six-hour clocks. She converted hours to minutes, minutes to seconds; surviving sheets record that 3600 seconds = 60 minutes = 1 hour. Carefully she drew in each second. Time was now something to play with. Fractional conversions became so rapid as to seem intuitive: 49 hours = $2\frac{1}{24}$ days. Soon she was mapping space as well as time: $7\frac{1}{2}$ inches = $\frac{5}{8}$ foot.

And hour after hour she multiplied and divided. There were no calculators then. I couldn't keep all the sheets of paper she consumed, and Jessy didn't want them. Once they were done, she'd internalized her discoveries, 51×51, 52×52, 53×53, and on and on. Even I could see what she was up to: determining squares, then cubes, then higher and higher powers. And what can be multiplied can be divided; her long division became more and more bizarre as she searched out larger primes and identified more factors. She liked the number 60; it was handy for clocks. I kept the sheet that said it was divisible twelve ways. But that was just the beginning. Months later another sheet recorded that 26082 was divisible by 1, 2, 3, 6, 7, 9, 14, 18, 21, 23, 27, 42, 46, 54, 63, 69, 81, 126, 138, 161, 162, 189, 207, 322, 378, 414, 483, 567, 621, 966, 1134, 1242, 1449, 1863, 2898. There the numbers stopped. Did she finish the series somewhere else?

Other sheets explored the factors of 13041 and 19380. Fractions too could be factored: 1½ is divisible by 1/100, 1/50, 3/100, 1/20, 3/50, 1/10, 3/20, 1/4, 1/2, 3/4, 1½. Though numbers were generally a solitary pastime, now and then we looked over them together. Jessy had written 2, 2, 2, 3, 5, 5, 7, 7. "If you multiply together you get 29400," she told me. On another sheet appeared 678586773483121410. When her father remarked it was not a prime, Jessy explained that it was "lots of primes multiplied together." Other numerical pastimes were less challenging. Jessy was happy counting to 10,000 by 100's, to 15,000 by 150's. Not very interesting, perhaps, but very autistic. Years later we met an Australian boy, far more advanced than Jessy, who spent his free time counting to a million, and I have seen sheets of primes and multiplications by Joseph Sullivan, one of the models for the Dustin Hoffman character in the movie *Rain Man,* that could easily be taken for Jessy's.

. . .

I can follow Jessy's math up to a point; primes and cubes and prime factors are not in fact all that complicated. But I know my limits. I quote again from Ron Ellis and Lola Bogyo, glad to reiterate what we owe to them and to all those who accompanied Jessy beyond what we could manage. "Many hands make light work" is one of Jessy's favorite proverbs.

By age 13 she could list, on request, all the prime numbers from 1 to 1000 and beyond. . . . Two prime integers . . . stood out among the rest: 7 . . . and 3. . . . [Jessy] endlessly explored the composites and combinations of these numbers. . . . She discovered, among many other things, that the delightful formal symmetry of the integer 10,001 could be generated unexpectedly by multiplying 73 × 137. This formal symmetry was used to produce integers possessing a duplicating structure, as in the following examples:

$$10001 \times 137 = 1370137$$
$$10001 \times 7003 = 70037003$$
$$10001 \times 7337 = 73377337$$

[Jessy] correctly inferred that she could generate formal duplication without directly using the integer 10001 but by embedding its factors in her calculations:

$$37 \times 37 = 1369$$
$$1369 \times 73 = 99937$$
$$99937 \times 137 = 13691369 \text{ (formal duplication)}$$

[Jessy] also found that she could encrypt selected integers within her duplicating structures by the formation of composites and then retrieve the original digits in a delightfully altered form by further manipulations:

$$13691369 \times 53 = 725642557 \text{ (53 is encrypted)}$$
$$725642557 + 37 = 19611961 \text{ (a formal duplication)}$$
$$19611961 \div 37 = 530053 \text{ (53 appears in duplicate!)}$$

. . . Wherever there were patterns, however complex or subtle, [Jessy] discovered them; wherever instances adhered to some underlying rule, that rule was induced. . . . She

4096 9216 6400 3136 5184
7744 2704 3600 4624 5776
7056 8464 10000 2916 3364 3844
4356 4900 5476 6084 6724 7396
8100 8836 9604 2601 2809 3025
3249 3481 3721 3969 4225
4489 4761 5041 5329 5625 5929
6241 6561 6889 7225 7569
7924 8281 8649 9025 9409 9801

It took a mathematician to unravel the system behind this series of numbers Jessy produced at age twelve.

explored her world of numbers until it had become predictable and ordered.[2]

That was impressive enough. But it took our friend Freeman Dyson of the Institute for Advanced Study in Princeton to recognize Jessy's most remarkable feat. The summer she turned twelve, Jessy produced sheet after sheet bearing the same strange series of fifty four-digit numbers. Or was it a series? It didn't look like one. There is no obvious relation between 4096, 9216, 6400, and 5184. Only a mathematician's eye would recognize that Jessy had arranged the squares of the numbers from 51 to 100 according to the number of powers of 2 they contain. 4096 is 64^2 or 2^{12}; it is made of nothing but 2's. 9216 is 96^2; 96 is 3×32, 32 is 2^5, and so on. The odd numbers, beginning with 2601, which is the square of 51, complete the list. (And since many hands do make work lighter, it is Jessy's father who deserves the credit for the wording of this explanation.)

. . .

To certain minds the language of mathematics is particularly attractive for its abstraction, for the beauty of pure idea, independent of human waywardness. And certainly that was one reason Jessy liked math. Yet the explanation is too simple, for as with clocks, many of Jessy's numbers had strong linkages to the world. Some of these were emotionally neutral. Back home three of the Jessy-friends were counting calories; she recorded their weights (111, 126, and 140) and multiplied them together for the impressive total. She factored numbers derived from the number of times her superball bounced on a given day. But many were emotionally charged; like clouds and sunshine they could bring misery or delight. We had never noticed that telephone poles are numbered, but Jessy had. If she missed one there were mumbles, or worse. As once with washcloths, Jessy could be desolated by the incomplete.

SOMEBODY ATE A PIECE OF THE SALAD
ONLY 399 PIECES IN A BOWL
I HAVE A COLD
$7256425570 = 5 \, 2/7 \times 1372837270$
I CRIED WHEN SOMEBODY ATE A PIECE OF
    THE SALAD

Though Jessy had typed answers to Megan's questions, these words, carefully printed in capitals, were almost her first spontaneous written communication. She was twelve. Every statement but the second was literally true, yet together they seemed meaningless. But they were not meaningless to Jessy. She had cried, she had *shrieked*. Then, alone in her room, she had expressed her anguish in words, and in numbers as bewildering as the cause of her distress. It was hard to forget that timeless wailing and remember her delight in the discovery that "70003 is a *prime!*"

Yet we had learned that numerical desolations, like others, were temporary. Later that year Jessy, having noted that 2730 was a HATE number, recorded its factors, as she had done in the past: 1, 2, 3, 5, 6, 7, 10, 13, 14, 15, 21, 26, 30, 35, 39, 42, 65, 70, 78, 91, 105, 130, 182, 195, 210, 273, 390, 455, 546, 910, 1365, 2730. But this time she added a comment: ITS CHAINGED TO GOOD. And suddenly time rolled backward; I realized why, three years earlier, not yet able to write, she'd drawn so many chains. As words and numbers connected, another window opened on that strange inner world.

. . .

All that was long, long ago. Jessy's math, though as accurate as ever, is now ordinary, real-world stuff, useful for balancing a checkbook or making out a tax form; fractional conversions are handy for baking. There are no more HATE numbers, and she has forgotten many of the primes and prime factors that she used to whisper because they were "too good." Numbers, like others of her obsessions, have, in her own phrase, "worn away," as she has entered more and more fully into the normal world of the everyday. And that itself is normal. How many of us leave an interest behind, or a skill, as the piano stands unopened or the sketchbooks gather dust?

And yet — how much there is in Jessy's mind we don't know about! A year ago her father and I were wondering why our home phone gave a continual busy signal; was it out of order? Jessy picked up on our conversation. (That itself is something she never used to do.) Unexpectedly she informed us that the out-of-order signal was like the busy signal but with 120 beeps per minute instead of 60. Now who knew that?

But counting may be only a habit when you've done it all your life. There are other indications that numbers persist, no longer emotion-filled, no longer secret, but underground. This year I notice that her social security number ends in 1421; I mention that (obviously) it's divisible by 7. It's even more obvious to Jessy; "Divisible by 7^2," she says. I recall another instance. Jessy had written 1875 in one of her old books and I asked her if she remembered anything about it. Though it was half her lifetime past, her answer was immediate. "Has a 3 in it. And 5^4." And indeed, divide it by 3 and you get 625: $5 \times 5 \times 5 \times 5$! It's no great surprise, then, to find she's factored the year of her birth: 1958 is 2×979. "979," she says, "is definitely a prime."

．　．　．

As I go over envelopes and slips I find an old calculation. $1988 = 2^2 \times 497$, $497 = 7 \times 71$. Jessy is interested in the book about her, and answers willingly when I ask her about 1998. Divided by 3^3 it equals 74, which divided by 2 gives (old faithful!) 37. I ask about 1999. It's early in the year and Jessy, ever truthful, says she's not sure about 1999. 1997? But by now she's had enough. What's past is past: "I'm too old," she says.

CHAPTER 7   "The hangman
hangs by the clothespin
because of new politeness"

Strangeness/Secret Life — a label on an envelope in a folder
crammed with other envelopes, Hypersensitivities, Obsessions,
Compulsions, and the rest. As if a folder, as if even a suitcase,
could contain the strangeness that suffused our family's every
day. Strange systems, strange numbers; still, I need another chapter to explore (not exhaust) the strangeness of that busy mind, the
bewildering interplay between its creativity and its handicap.

The contents of the suitcase are spread all over my bedroom as
I try to classify and select. Drawings of "little imitation people."
"Books," hundreds of them; there were months when she made
one almost every day. As her language progressed she titled them:
Book About the Number with Three in It; Book About the
Number *of* Three in It; Book About the Bump; Book About
the Light in the Science Building; Book About the Shadow.
The records of her preoccupations, her enjoyments, her anxieties,
her desolations. I have been in no hurry to put them away, think-
ing she would be interested in these relics of past absorptions.
In the years when talking — and human interaction — was an

educational project, the best way to elicit speech was to revisit this library of former experience. Her books were made for her own satisfaction, not to communicate experience but to record it. Still, she would explain if we asked the right questions and we didn't press too hard. Though intentional, eager communication ("Come see!") lay far in the future, the books, with their successive layers of explanations, allowed us glimpses of the world within.

She wouldn't — couldn't — say much about her books in the early years, often not more than a few garbled words. But I'd write them down. A year or two later, returning to the same book, I could gauge how much her language had progressed, when she now had the words to clarify the explanations that had been a puzzle. I'd write those down too.

Jessy remembered then and she remembers now. Briefly the books about the numbers catch her interest; she wants to explain the "difference between 'with' and 'of'." "Of" means divisible by 3; "with" means there is an actual 3 to be seen. But she looks no further. It's I who am interested. This is the past; she has better things to do.

The little imitation people came first, inspired by the illustrations for *Gulliver's Travels* and *The Borrowers*. Before she understood words, I was always drawing for her, showing her pictures. We looked at *The Treasury of Art Masterpieces;* we looked at the nice explicit illustrations in beginning readers. We looked at *Harold and the Purple Crayon,* where what Harold draws with his crayon becomes his own story. And the year she turned nine she too began to draw her own stories and enter them. The books began.

The first were the series of what Jessy called "comic books." Harold and his crayon provided both inspiration and model; Jessy's

Jessy's "little imitation people."

adventures followed his closely. TV was another source; Batman appeared, and renditions of TV logos — NBC, ABC — and true to form, nonsense acronyms, VBC, ZBC, KBC. Jessy was now interested enough in letters to use them. Mysterious words appeared — not words she might be expected to know, like "cake," but GAKE, VAKE, GOKE, day after day. More nonsense, we thought — until, years later, she explained those as the noise of the heat coming on in the radiator and we understood why she had refused to enter rooms where she might hear the offending sound. Sometimes, however, the secret life remained secret. "Not for Mama. Oh oh, do *not* look at any more pictures, please!" and she crumpled it up and threw it away. Enough was enough.

Jessy was quite conscious of her sources. "This is all from Bat-man." I never understood the Batman plot, which involved two tigers, a fight, and a fall in the water. But the progression was orderly, the drawings clearly sequential. If the characters climbed a hill on one page, on the next they descended, or ("like Harold!") they fell from it, their streaming hair obeying gravity to register their fall. I had made her figures out of pipe cleaners, and Piper Cleaner Man, Piper Cleaner Lady, Piper Cleaner Girl and Boy, Piper Cleaner Fairy — and Paper Doll Jessy — formed the basic cast, occasionally joined by Big Girl Jessy, Mama, and Daddy. Piper Cleaner people came and went mysteriously, Jessy keeping careful count. Sometimes she doubled the group, and there would be two Paper Doll Jessies as well. The cast increased as she grew more interested in numbers: twelve, sixteen, eighteen, twenty-one.

The next year numbers took over. An isolated sheet shows the numbers from 0 to 8, drawn hollow so a corresponding number of Piper Cleaner people could cavort with Jessy inside each one. (The zero, of course, is empty.) Then Piper Cleaners became rare, replaced by row after row of standing figures whose bodies are actual numbers. There are odd consistencies; the hair on each 5 figure — 5, 15, 50 — always stands on end, and there is always a 200-person, often Jessy herself, to remind us that that busy mind knew exactly what it was doing, even if we didn't.[1]

Jessy's simple plots were uniformly upbeat. Paper Doll Jessy may open a door and fall into water (bubbles rising), but she finds another door, a rope, and returns to the Piper Cleaner family. The Piper Cleaners, naturally thin, procure sticks of gum and grow fat. If, as in Batman, they fight, the fight is "for fun." If they fall, they and Paper Doll Jessy still proceed home, to end safely in her bed, or occasionally with a party. That was natural enough;

Harold's adventures ended happily too. But the next year, when she'd done with Piper Cleaner books, *Slovenly Peter* hardly encouraged so benign a vision. Heinrich Hoffmann's verses for bad children can raise the hair on an ordinary child. But Jessy made a book of two of the worst; in one a cry-baby literally cries her eyes out, in the other a hyperactive boy romps so hard he breaks off his foot. The German illustrator showed the detached foot and the two eyes on the floor, and so did Jessy. In her version, however, "ring a bell, girl and dog come" to restore the eyes and bring another foot. "Put the foot on, stand up!" In other books poor families are given meat, new houses, and finally a Christmas tree. Even a book about a terrifying night-long lightning storm ends with Jessy peacefully in bed, the storm over and a cerulean blue window heralding the dawn.

. . .

But the child's world of happy endings was coming to an end. Numbers could turn bad. Flavor tubes and weather anxieties lay ahead. And Jessy, entering adolescence, was more and more engaged in the human world. We were glad of that. But the human world is not Nirvana. Her family, her companions, her teachers, had been endlessly patient, but "endlessly" is all too easily written. No one's patience is endless, and one expects more from a fourteen-year-old, even from a handicapped fourteen-year-old, than from a child. Not everyone — *no one* — can stand everything all the time. It is not always possible to call on emotional reserves when so much effort, so much affection, is rewarded only with a hostile "Go away!" Though anger is always regrettable, it is more than rationalization to recognize that it may convey, in the only way it *can* be conveyed, the important social knowledge that people do have limits, that actions can have unpleasant consequences, and that there are good reasons to undertake the hard work of self-control.

Nirvana was increasingly under siege. It had been a long time coming, but Jessy, now thirteen, was at last in her local public school — not for a short morning but for a full school day, with teachers who, however bewildered (few had even heard of autism then), tried every way they could think of to teach. It wasn't easy, for them or for Jessy. There were bells that outraged autistic ears, demands that infringed autistic aloneness, changes that disturbed the autistic routines that kept her world in order. At home, though banshee shrieking could be more than we could bear we had learned to bear it; school could not be so tolerant. At home there was no boundary between teaching and play, we knew her capacities and kept within them; she knew little of the frustration of failure, and lessons stopped when her attention wandered or she refused to answer. Now there were errors that must be corrected, scoldings when she veered into nonsense or something set her dreaming. "Why are you smiling?" We had played for years at reading and writing; now she must work.

Jessy's books from these years are very different. I did not realize how different until I emptied the suitcase and found nine different Books About the Bump. As Jessy explained later, "Somebody bump me, hit me, kick me back." Because she did kick people sometimes, and hit them too. And she was hit. A schoolmate bumped her. A companion bumped her "because I scribbled." Her sister bumped her "because I threw a tantrum." Her father bumped her. I bumped her. And each bump was memorialized in a book.

Rooted not in derivative and stereotyped plots but in daily experience, the books of Jessy's adolescence were far more creative than the books of childhood. Page numbers were pressed

into self-expression: she designed a font of "silly-looking" numbers for bad days, contrasting with "fancy numbers" for good
days and "a little bit fancy for fairly good day and regular day I
wrote down a regular number." Grotesquely tall and narrow, bad
numbers reached from top to bottom of a large page, while
bumper and bumpee climbed up a 2 or hung from a distorted 3.
The title of one book was made entirely out of small leaves, gath-
ered for the purpose and carefully taped down. In another, every
letter of both title and the final THE END was itself composed
of neatly lettered BUMP's, in another, of 70003's.

Some books were neutral records of events — there are three
about local fires. But more typical were the books about anxieties
or obsessions. There are three books about seeing the light in the
science building. In the books Jessy kicks the building; at home
she screamed and screamed. Shadows were an obsession of an
opposite kind. They were "too good" to walk through — she had
to squinch her eyes shut — and there are many books in which
shadows, of buildings, of furniture, of numbers, even of stick figures, are shown with a startling realism.

Though most drawings are in ink or pencil, one is striking for
its color. Jessy wrote Book About the Shadow when she was fourteen. The first three words are in her newly acquired cursive.
SHADOW, however, is in my capitals; it was "too good" for her
to write. The shadow of the penciled house on the cover is "too
good" indeed, its emotional intensity conveyed by a surreal harmony of concentric rectangles in shades of blue and lavender and
green. Inside pages (with "fancy numbers") show nine different
buildings with their shadows, each as it appeared on a particular
date at a particular time of day. All are done from memory; three
years later she supplied the dates and times. Usually Jessy appears
alone, eyes tight shut, walking in the shadow. In one drawing,

however, I am with her. She, not I, recalled that building in a distant city, and how we walked through its shadow together. But I know when we took that trip, and her date is correct. I am glad it was a good day, and that no cloud covered the sun. "I used to care about that. It was important for me having a good day. It isn't anymore."

There were other good days. Stars were becoming "too good," and Thanksgiving 1971 produced a Book About the Star, a star enclosing each page number. On one page a bowl of star-filled soup is set ready, each bit of chicken and carrot carefully colored in. "Chicken and stars mean too good to eat."

But another book for a good day shows the peculiar doubleness that haunted Jessy's obsessions. The Book About the Record was "good because I heard the song called 'The Hangman'" and the hangman was good — too good, as we were to learn. Page numbers are fancy, and both title and THE END are made of phonograph records. The drawings show a record player as its tone arm progresses through the record's two sides. The hangman song is on side 2, but the record could bring sadness as well as pleasure. "I used to fuss about not hearing the first three songs on side one."

It was the hangman that inspired the most arresting of Jessy's pictures, one of thirty-two made on a companion's suggestion that she illustrate each of the songs they sang together. To see the rendition of "God gave Noah the rainbow sign" is to realize the meaning of autistic literalism; on a signpost is an actual sign, striped with the rainbow. But it is the illustration for "Hangman" that grips the attention. Against a purple sky, a figure, flesh-colored, naked, hangs on a brown cross. His large eyes are wide open, and startlingly blue. Jessy had not forgotten the crucifixions in *The Treasury of Art Masterpieces,* but "Hangman" is not about Jesus. "Hangman, hangman, slack your rope, slack it for a while. I think I see my mother comin', comin' from many a mile." Jessy

Pages from the Book About the Shadow.

The rainbow sign.

drew no hooded executioner, no "gallows pole"; she knew nothing of these things. The hangman is quite simply a man who hangs, as a rainbow sign is a sign.

The hangman song was good in the Book About the Record; in the Book About the Songs it was weirdly neutral. But there was trouble ahead. A hangman might hang on a cross. He might hang on a tree. He might hang on a clothesline, suspended from an accurately drawn clothespin. He might not hang at all, but skip and jump, depending on . . . well, what it depended on was so strange that it requires a paragraph to itself.

The hangman, drawn to illustrate a favorite song.

For years we had tried to get Jessy to say "please" and "thank you." As she grew older we tried harder: good manners are even more important for a handicapped person than for the rest of us. Jessy hated to say "thank you." She would overcome her resistance for birthdays and Christmas, shutting her eyes and rushing the words out as fast as she could. Soon she reacted to the very sound of what she called "politenesses." She would refuse to offer a guest a plate of cookies, lest she should hear a "no thank you." A "late politeness" could ignite a full-blown tantrum, while the bewildered guest wondered what he'd done wrong. "The hangman makes a sad face and this makes me go wild."

"Every time there is a late politeness hangman will hang on the tree and every time a mistaken politeness" — I still don't know what that might be — "hangman will skip around. How about latest politeness ever? Hangman will hang on the largest tree. How about late mistaken? First skip around and then hang! How about high politeness?" (I.e., spoken in a high voice.) "Hangman will jump way up high."

In short, a system; her drawing shows eight levels of late and/or mistaken politenesses in which eight color-coordinated hangmen jump higher and higher on successively bigger trees. A late "you're welcome" has its own picture. "The hangman hangs by the clothespin because of new politeness." Jessy, who had understood so few words, was now verbally alert — in her way. On the drawing she lettered YOU'RE SO WELCOME, YOU'RE QUITE WELCOME, YOU'RE VERY WELCOME, YOU'RE MOST WELCOME, YOU'RE SURELY WELCOME, YOU'RE CERTAINLY WELCOME, YOU'RE MOST CERTAINLY WELCOME, and YOU'RE MORE THAN WELCOME. Eventually she told us why she didn't like politenesses, why she had to shut her eyes. It was so she wouldn't see the hangman, there in my eyes, in anybody's eyes, hanging on a pole.

· · ·

Obsessive-compulsive disorder is a diagnosis; it is not usually thought of as a kind of thinking. In Jessy, however, obsessions and compulsions supplied both the material and the method of thought. Her systems, her numbers, her elaborate correlations, were integral to the activity of her mind. I don't know how neatly Jessy's array of strangenesses fit into the obsessive-compulsive box. Sometimes they seem too strange for any box but her own. Yet it seems a good enough label, though we've managed to get by without the drugs that are prescribed for it and that might indeed have made those hard times easier. Categories bleed; diagnoses in a given individual may never quite fit. Hypersensitivities, Obsessions, Compulsions — let the label, then, be a convenient shorthand for the oddities of thought, and feeling, and behavior that Jessy and we lived with.

Can an obsession make you happy? "I had a good time in school today because there was construction in a picture." At seventeen, the very thought made her smile — and draw her own picture of "layers of road which has three different layers of tar." Obsessions can certainly make you sad — along with everybody around you. Colds in the family make Jessy sad, for a very practical reason; she's afraid she'll catch one. We've learned to hide our symptoms as long as we can, for though she hates colds, she loves to talk about them. She'll rehearse the dates and circumstances of each of our colds years after they should have been forgotten — tedious talk, *obsessive* talk, talk that can have the effect of the Chinese water torture, especially when you've got a cold.

. . .

Most of her obsessions showed this doubleness. Pleasure might turn to pain; "too good" meant you couldn't stand it. Bad remembered might bring pleasure, as she laughed about the very thing that had set her crying. What more satisfying than to recall past distress? By the time she was in her twenties she made no more books, but she spent hours on listing her "discouragements" — five pages, twenty-two items with numbered subdivisions in proper outline form. "5. Run away if the refrigerator turns on after or while the door is opened, both bother me." "6. Discouragements at work": "Making errors while working," "Writing down wrong price and pressing wrong keys on the calculator," "Putting a piece of mail in the wrong box, wrong names in the right box, and repeating boxes after somebody already fill them." She's bothered by "being helped while working"; a coworker is all too likely to "mix hundreds, like 2471 mixed with 2500s and 3071 mixed with 3100s." These are the kinds of things that can (but today seldom do) cause her to "cry silently" at her desk, only to erupt as soon as she is on her way home for lunch. Today this rarely happens. Still troublesome, however, is number 7, "Questions that bother me."

A. What questions. What? What are you making? What are you doing?
B. Who questions. Who is somebody. I try to prevent them by identify people's names.
C. Questions of happiness. Why are you smiling? I don't like them, because they are too good to answer.

A couple of years later Jessy annotated her list, with characteristic precision. Her aversion to being helped was "outworked by fall 1986," number mix-ups "reduced a bit by 1987." Last year, rereading this list, Jessy made a philosophical comment. "This is what my life like. Like anything can be worn away and replaced by new things. Bad or good things. Like good things and discouragements both worn away." Jessy no longer makes a fuss if I forget to take one of the pills she so carefully counts out for me each morning; she can make sure I take it at lunch. She's more anxious if it rolls under the fridge; she's anxious if *anything* is missing, and if she hasn't noticed, we don't tell her. Because if we do, she'll go on and on and on about it, reminding us yet again that her brain is simply not good at switching from one channel to another. Lucky that a helper gave her the phrase "Drop it like a hot potato!" She thinks it's funny, and if we say it loud and sudden and with a laugh, it can break the connection so she too can laugh and move on.

But only a very few of these discouragements are completely "outworked." Jessy comes back from checking the boiler in the cellar. (Compulsiveness can be a valuable characteristic when tasks must be done regularly, and we need never fear that Jessy will forget to change the batteries in the smoke alarm.) In winter checking the boiler is routine, but today is different. Her face is radiant. She's made such strides in self-control that I feel I can take a risk. I don't ask "Why are you smiling?" but I approximate it. "What a happy face!" I say, hugging her. She accepts it, still smiling; she even answers the question she hears beneath my paraphrase. "The dryer going." "You like that?" "Yes — because of things going round and round!" But we're not home free. "I did get annoyed about that. I smiled about the dryer going" — and she begins to whimper, almost cry. But that's all this time — it's over, it's OK. That what our life like, tears and sunshine mixed. Yet Jessy insists on accentuating the positive. When a friend asked her what was her favorite obsession, he was told in no uncertain terms, "*All* obsessions are good!"

. . .

We read often that autistic children are deficient in imagination, in "pretend play." "Current diagnostic schemes pay particular attention to the abnormal lack of imaginative activity." "The lack of creative play [is] as unique and universal a feature . . . as [is] communication and socialization failure."[2] Few who have watched a child repeat the same sterile lineup over and over will disagree. Grown older, autistic people who read tend not to read novels, with their confusing representations of a social world that is confusing already. Secure in the stability of fact, they navigate poorly among fictions.

Yet what about Jessy's little imitation people? About her house plans with tiny steps so they can reach the china cupboard that is their "hotel"? "They rent different rooms in the hotel, just about a dollar a month. Sometimes they have slumber parties. A long time ago they used to live in the summer house but they moved during fall in 1972." What about the "make-believe forest where the Piper Cleaner family went during the party"?

"Make-believe" — exactly so. Jessy has always been quite clear about what is make-believe and what is real. (She was nine when she drew herself, Big Girl Jessy, crayon in hand, holding what was clearly her own drawing of a Piper Cleaner person — see page 178.) Often anxious, she was never fearful; real fear requires imagination. Jessy was immune to the usual fears; we used to think of her as the child in the fairy tale who didn't know how to shudder. There were no monsters under her bed. She was never afraid of the dark; it was the neighbor who was concerned when he found her sitting alone, lights out, one evening when her father and I were elsewhere. She wasn't upset by blood; at twelve, when her periods began she was exultant that what was predicted had occurred: "Blood *did* come!" Though today she is a regular blood donor, her satisfaction has little to do with altruism. "Into the small tube! It was fast! How fast! Too good to see! That's why I'm closing my eyes!"

There were dragons in her picture books, but Jessy did not imagine what dragons might do. She did not imagine what dangers might lurk in the dark. Blood did not make her think of wounds and death but of a regular appointment and a heart-shaped sticker. Menstruation was simply something that was supposed to come and did; she did not imagine the social anxieties of puberty. And yet she imagined the little people. Little imitation people, flavor tubes, elaborate, proliferating systems — so many glimpses of what a flawed but vigorous mind may create when, barred from ordinary experience, its energy flows into the limited channels of its comprehension.

· · ·

We had no idea of encouraging imagination when we drew so much with her, looked at so many pictures with her, filled her room with dolls and doll clothes and doll furniture. The absence of pretend play was not yet a diagnostic indicator, far from it; in the Bettelheim orthodoxy autistic children suffered from too *much* imagination, from noxious and terrifying hallucinations they could not distinguish from reality. We were just doing whatever we could think of to enrich her life. Jessy might line the dolls up on the dollhouse roof, as later she would line up her number people, but at least she wasn't sifting silly business.

But looking back over the record of Jessy's early years, I am struck by how often our groping play was, in fact, teaching her to pretend and enjoy it. Jessy was four when her father pretended to put her to bed on the kitchen floor. She was six when her siblings amused themselves getting her to mime them as they "died"; she learned it was fun to gag and choke and collapse on the rug. She'd laugh when her sister played "sad" with crocodile tears, though she knew what crying was. She might line up her dolls, but she gave them names, and once I even heard her tell one to "Eat up, dolly!" Recent work with autistic children shows that though pretend play, like other social behaviors, doesn't develop spontaneously, it can be taught.[3] Unconsciously we taught it, making the little people possible, making it possible for Jessy to think and say, years later, "Pretend the sun is the parent and the planets are the children and the earth is me!"

Nevertheless, the limitations of autism remained. The Piper Cleaner family were dependent on Batman and Harold for their activities; a year passed, and they were still enacting the same plots. The little people who later lived in our appliances, having no such originals, had no plots. Instead they had elaborate kinship structures, inspired by our lessons on the shifting words for family relationships and by the families of people she knew. "Guess what! The oven is a make-believe family also! Noise of the oven same as the buzzer of the washing machine. This part of the family has only two children and both get married and one of them has children and the other don't. And there are four parts of the family. Remember our family has two parts. Second part are my cousins. Stove has three sets of cousins. Some of the sisters and cousins are Karens. There are two Karens in two different sets of cousins and both didn't get married. Too young."

They were lovely to think about. But they *did* nothing, didn't go anywhere, even to bed or a party. Lorna Wing's generalization held good: "imaginative activities," while not, as in some cases, "totally absent," were "copied from other[s]," or "spontaneous but carried out repetitively or in an identical fashion."[4] Jessy couldn't invent. She could only combine — sometimes in startling ways — what she found elsewhere. Ten years ago I was astonished when she said, "I want to tell what it look like when I am imagining things" — astonished and hopeful. Would she, could she, at last open the window on that mysterious interior? But her next words disabused me: "I saw it on cartoons!"

. . .

Strange hypersensitivities, strange obsessions, strange compulsions, strange, explosive reactions. Strangeness can be frightening, especially when it lunges at you suddenly, loudly, hostilely, even with violence. As recently as the seventies, children like Jessy were called psychotic, and the terms "autism" and "childhood schizophrenia" were used interchangeably. In the long centuries before those labels, there was another explanation for such children. We found out what it was when a religious acquaintance told us that there are (still!) church rituals for casting out demons, and that we should have Jessy exorcised. I have seen Jessy's father really angry only once, on the day it was suggested that his little daughter was in the power of the devil.

So I revert from the dark side of Jessy's strangeness to what was, and is, far more characteristic, to her quirky, innocent pleasures. "Anna's dishwasher sounds like *music,* even run nonstop like music running nonstop. General Electric don't stop!" She rocks in pure delight.

There is pleasure in transition phrases on the TV. There is pleasure in the fivefold division of Route 7 (including its extension north as Route 133 in Canada). There is pleasure in "astrothings," especially anything to do with Venus, like the shell on which she rises from the waves in *The Treasury of Art Masterpieces*. "I saw Vena ["Venus" is too good to say] peeping out at the corner of the science building." Anything that ends in *-nus* is good — not only Uranus and Cygnus, but minus and Janus and bonus as well. Why? Because NUS is "the greater light backwards," the greater light of Genesis 1, a.k.a. "the great big identified nonflying object," as Jessy grabs at any means to suppress that too-good word. Her world is full of "enthusiasms," which is what she calls these strange sources of delight. "There are many different kinds of happinesses," she tells me. "Enthusiasms, ecstasies, encouragement, enjoyment, bubbly. Joy!"

PART THREE

Painting

Jessy Park: *Merrill Lynch & Godiva at the World Financial Center,* 1999.

CHAPTER 8

"The sky is purple-black"

Jessy's in her room, the door shut. I knock of course — the proper behavioral lesson — but it's years since we heard the angry "Go away!" of her adolescence. Today, though, there's a pause before the "Come in." I know why; she's doing "secrets," and she's putting them away. Though the tubes of acrylics are in place, her table is empty of its usual work-in-progress. It's three weeks before Christmas — or Valentine's Day, or Easter — and Jessy is painting her little cards. Each family member will get one; so will former Jessy-helpers; so will the "housemates" who live with her when we are away.

It's a happy task. The holiday itself is happy to think about, and her chosen subject matter makes it happier still. Twenty years of little cards adorn our kitchen, the multicolored record of Jessy's "enthusiasms," her obsessions, unalloyed by the lurking anxieties that lie in ambush for them in real life.

Each 3-by-5 card is a miniature painting. There are double-yolked eggs. There's a whole series of astrothings — solar eclipses, lunar eclipses, the planets in full array. There's Venus rising, so bright that it casts a shadow. There's a horizon with a green flash. There are five bees, safely dead. A monarch butterfly is so exquisitely detailed it seems real. A tomato hornworm recalls Jessy's first pun, and her happy laugh when the hornworm blew its horn.

Time passes; enthusiasms "wear away" and new ones succeed them. No more astrothings, but houses, all sorts of houses. That was the period — it lasted more than a year — when Jessy, her voice tense with pleasure, would tell you, "I'm interested in *real estate!*" And she was, but not the way other people are interested in real estate; the economics of it meant nothing to her. Rather, her interest was in classification for its own sake. The phrase "starter house" made her shiver with delight. She would go on and on about "luxury homes," "million-dollar homes," though that was a category, not a price, determined not by grandeur of grounds or architecture, but (of course) the number of bedrooms, baths, and half-baths. And now, banks . . .

But other cards are less autistic, more sociable, as Jessy learns to look for subjects that are appropriate to their recipients. There are cat portraits for her cat-loving sister. Her Scottish brother-in-law, born in Glasgow on St. Patrick's Day, gets a four-leaf clover for his birthday, for Christmas (my suggestion) the Glasgow city seal. The real estate enthusiasm itself grew out of actual conversations with her friend Anna about the purchase of a starter house. Like her books, her little cards show a progression, unsteady but real, toward engagement with the ordinary world.

.   .   .

What's art is a matter of definition. "Those are the cookie art," Jessy said of her SING-SANG-SUNG collage. She never applied that term to her books. The Book About the Shadow, about the troubling Light, were in another category, one she could recog-

Shadows cast by the number 78, and by the stick figure of Jessy herself.

nize though she couldn't name it. They were functional records; that was why, I think, she seldom bothered with color, why she took no trouble with her drawing, except when an obsessive anxiety called forth the eerie realism of the science building or the shadow cast by an enormous 78. Color was for beauty, I think, though Jessy wouldn't have said that either. So she cut out school menus and painted them and pasted them up in pastel strips; she made collages with multicolored silly business and crumpled tissue paper and her own name in string. The books were important, but I don't think the farthest-out critic would call them art, still less apply the term to the illustrations for the journals she's kept intermittently since the books were abandoned. As drawings, there is nothing remarkable about them except that they were the drawings of an autistic child and are now the drawings of an autistic adult. Jessy was four when she drew her first crude representation of a human being. She was nine when the comic books began. And since that time her representations of human figures have not changed at all.

It is remarkable when an adolescent, still more an adult, still more an adult who has been taught to draw, draws like a child. Paul Klee did not, for all his attraction to children's art; more precisely, he could not. Nothing is more difficult than to draw like a child unless you are one. I would say impossible, except that Jessy does it. I watch her as for the ten-thousandth time she makes a circle for the head, an oval for the unclothed body, single short strokes for each arm and leg. Only the hair differentiates individuals; hers is straight, mine curls, boys and men have none. The whole figure is done in less time than she'd take to write it. In fact she *is* writing it. It's clear what these are: not drawings but ideograms, conventional, rapid, unvarying. They have nothing in common with her renditions of buildings or her portraits.

Those portraits are surprisingly skillful, considering that there are so few of them — no more than can be counted on the fingers of one hand. She made them in 1973. Ask her today if she'd draw a person and she'll say no: "too hard." But then it was different. The portraits were set assignments. Anna and Diana were teaching her to draw.

The twins met Jessy in art class. As she entered high school, art (like gourmet cooking and, later, business math) was something she could take with normal children. It didn't take long for the teachers to discover that this bizarre youngster who screamed at the bells and scratched in the wrong places and could hardly talk could do any assignment given the normal teenagers. She could do a still life with a flag and a bottle, she could render the same subject cubistically . . . *if* she understood that that was what she was supposed to do. So it was that Anna and Diana entered her life. Fascinated by the paradox of someone nearly their own age who acted like a four-year-old when she wasn't acting worse, yet could draw anything set in front of her, they appointed themselves interpreters between her and the busy teachers. They were among the few who could draw better than she could, and they decided to *really* teach her to draw. They didn't go for cubism or weird subject matter. Theirs was the tried and true method of the Renaissance workshops, and it was exactly right for a person with autism; they made model drawings and had her copy them. There was nothing "creative" about their assignments, nothing expressive. Once or twice people had tried to get Jessy to draw a "happy" or "sad" picture; she had no idea what they wanted of her. The twins were concrete, definite; they told her firmly what to do and she did it. They set her subjects she never would have chosen — flowers, interiors, even those portraits. She developed a line of exquisite sureness; a drawing of Anna seated (reproduced in *The Siege*) looks almost like a Matisse. Only the date makes it credible that it comes from the same year as the last of her books. A portrait of her father is an instantly recognizable likeness, of him as well as of the wicker chair he sits in — while in the foreground looms a large bare foot. It's Jessy's own, there in the drawing as it was in her line of vision as she sat opposite him on the bed. What child of five has not absorbed the social knowledge that you don't include your foot in a picture of your father? But Jessy drew what she saw. It is the mind, not the eye, that selects.

Jessy's portrait of her father, done in her teens, about the same time as the 78 drawing.

The twins taught her academic drawing, and year after year, for the nine years she remained in high school, the teachers taught her too. When Anna and Diana went off to college, Jessy, unless in school, rarely took up a pencil.

Or a brush. For before the twins got to work, Jessy had had another teacher. Valerie was a painter. Jessy had painted in nursery school — repetitive triangles, squares, zigzags — abstract patterns, oddly neat for a small child, balanced, controlled, *composed*. She had paints at home — she understood that red and white make pink before I told her — but unless I set them up she preferred the ease of crayons, using them to draw, not to color. But Valerie had acrylics, and acrylics are quick-drying, as easy to use as the poster paints of nursery school. With Val's encouragement, Jessy's colors — and her obsessions — bloomed into glory. That summer's recurrent theme was Dutch elm disease, three trees healthy and one afflicted, a background of greens and blues and rich reds, or stars and rainbows, or the variously rayed sun. But Valerie lived with us only one summer. It would be years before Jessy would — except on assignment — paint again.

. . .

Even while admiring Jessy's increasing competence, we mourned the vanished strangeness. But the art of normal children, too, loses its freshness when the demands of realism take over, and few children regain it. Perhaps, we reflected, we should welcome Jessy's academic realism as normal development, not regret it as a sacrifice. After all, we had no plans to make her into an artist.

We couldn't have guessed how time, and luck, would bring everything together — luck and the principle of numerical reinforcement. We took Jessy to an autism meeting where I was making a speech. She was already twenty-one, too old for the children's activities provided, and I suggested she sketch to keep her busy. She made an accurate, ugly sketch of the ugly building we were meeting in, a man who'd heard my speech offered five dollars for it, and that's what started her career. A later chapter will describe how in her teenage years she'd worked for "points" to build skills and improve behavior. Money worked the same way. For years she had had no *reason* to paint or draw. Concepts of creativity or fame, of course, were meaningless. Money didn't mean much more. But numbers did, and she liked to see them rise in her checkbook. The staff at the Society for Autistic Children were very kind; they gave her a little exhibition, and sketches and school paintings were sold for small sums. The glorious colors began to come back, and then to proliferate. Perhaps she remembered a school exercise from years before, when she had been told to paint a snow scene, first in its natural white and evergreen, then in whatever colors fantasy might suggest. Who knows? At any rate, Jessy was drawing again, not because she was told to but because she wanted to. Once more she was finding her own subject matter. She drew, then painted, not snow landscapes, still less portraits or even buildings; she drew radio dials, speedometers and mileage gauges, clocks, heaters, and electric blanket controls. People with autism like such things. Jessy's fascination gave these new paintings an intensity that her academic drawings had lacked. Not that these weren't realistic, but a dial is more than a dial when it is realized in apricot and turquoise. Jessy's dials and gauges dazzled; her heaters throbbed with color as in a dream, transfiguring the simple grid perceived by her geometrizing eye. Sometimes they achieved an instant surrealism; what more natural than to honor three enthusiasms together? So against an electric blue she combined a rock group logo, an album title, and a heater, to yield the bizarrerie of *Boekamp Heater with Women and Children First*.

Electric blanket controls, in an untitled painting by Jessy.

Jessy had reverted to the abstract patterns of her childhood. But now they were abstractions in the true sense — patterns perceived in, drawn from, *abstracted* from, the visible world. There was a window in a house near us; through it, by some architectural quirk, a chimney could be seen, right up against the glass. Fascinated by the pattern of the bricks, Jessy painted it four times: first just the chimney; then the chimney and the window; then chimney, window, and roof; finally chimney, window, roof, and the night sky with stars.

Jessy Park: *Dagmar's House with Chimney in the Window,*
1984.

People liked the dials and heaters; if we'd lived in New York
they'd have gone over big as pop art. But art, for an autistic person, can be a vehicle of social learning. Jessy had already learned,
reluctantly, that people won't buy just anything, that she had to
put time into her work; now she learned that though people like
dials and heaters, most of them prefer houses, trees, and stars. She

had begun to spend hours poring over the *Field Guide to the Stars;* astronomy was a new obsession. Jessy wanted to paint a starry sky, but she didn't know how she could paint the house and the chimney when everything was dark. She needed the support of tactful suggestion — tactful, for she had become very sensitive to what she perceived as criticism. Honoring surrealism and strangeness, her father showed her Magritte's painting of an evening street scene against a bright sunny sky; reversing Magritte, she could keep the house in the daylight yellow of her earlier versions and *still* have stars above. So she painted the sky "purple-black," and Orion with Betelgeuse and Rigel in their correct colors and magnitudes, and Venus. A friend saw it and wanted one like it. Of course Jessy could have made another chimney in the window; she never minded repetition. But we suggested she tailor it to her client, an astronomer specializing in the Southern Hemisphere. So Jessy painted the professor's house with the Magellanic Cloud and the Southern Cross, and from then on her path was clear.

· · ·

That was almost twenty years ago, and art has continued to make its contribution to Jessy's social education. Back then she was indifferent to praise of her paintings; now she smiles in pleasure. She likes it when people come to see her work. She can tolerate the interruption; she can even tolerate making one of the mistakes she calls a "painto," a word she invented on the analogy of "typo" (to be joined immediately by "cooko," "bake-o," and "speako"). Paintos used to elicit the banshee wail, even when they could be fixed easily with a stroke of the brush. It's not the ease of repair that counts if you're autistic, it's the simple fact of error, in a world that seems controllable only when things go exactly according to plan.

PAINTING

Exactly; that's the word. There is no vagueness in her painting, no dashing brushwork, no atmospheric washes. It's hard-edge stuff; it always has been. No impressionism for Jessy, and no expressionism either. Even in nursery school she never over-lapped one color on another, never scrubbed them together into lovely, messy mud. There were no free splashes, no drips, no fin-ger paints. Her very first paintings were as autistic as these today.

Her art is autistic in other ways too. Autistic literalism has its visual equivalent; Jessy's eye acts like a camera. Should we be sur-prised? Jessy is the seventh autistic person to come to my atten-tion who drew in perspective before the age of eight. Perspective drawing seems to us a mark of artistic sophistication; we know that European artists did not master it until the Renaissance. Yet if we consider art historian E. H. Gombrich's insight that the nor-mal child draws not what it sees but what it knows — not its per-ception of the thing but the idea of the thing — we need not wonder at the ability of some autistic people to draw in perspec-tive, even when severely retarded. Cameras do not ponder, they record.

And there is the lack of shading. Only in the last ten years has Jessy learned to gradually alter an expanse of color to make it seem to recede or appear round. Even so, most of her colors remain flat. Indeed, that unsettling tension between the prevail-ing flatness and the few bits of round is part of what makes her realism surreal. No shading. No nuance. Like her speech. Like her simplified comprehension of what people say, of their expres-sions, their emotions and needs. I recall the autistic man who when asked of six test photos of faces, "How do they feel?" replied, "Soft." There is no shading in the way Jessy apprehends the world. Nuance *means* shading. Call it a metaphor of her autism, or more than a metaphor.

But if Jessy's painting bespeaks her handicap, it is a handicap not surmounted but transmuted into something rich and strange. Here is autism in its core characteristics, literal, repetitive, obsessively exact — yet beautiful. In her paintings, reality has been transfigured. Who wouldn't want a painting of their house, recognizable to the last detail, but shimmering in colors no householder could conceive? Especially when they can get their favorite constellation thrown in?

I should not, however, allow a metaphor to engulf all autistic art. Stephen Wiltshire, the best-known autistic artist, also has a camera eye, but he makes little use of color, and his fine draftsmanship is as free as Jessy's is controlled.[1] Mark Rimland works in delicate watercolor washes. Individuals are individuals as well as autistic. Jessy has her own obsessions, her own style, her own family, her own genetics. She's good at numbers. Her father is a theoretical physicist. She can draw. So can I, and her grandfather was a painter. Would she have been a painter — or a mathematician — if she had not been autistic? Who can say how heredity and environment and disability come together?

Nevertheless, the autistic art I have seen has strong commonalities. Buildings are a common subject, and usually one can see every brick. Often these are done from memory, as Jessy drew the science building. Often they are seen from above, or some other viewpoint the artist cannot possibly have occupied. Usually there is characteristic subject matter; one woman obsessively draws traffic lights as people. And there is a characteristic absence; like Jessy, they are unlikely to choose to make portraits. "Too hard." Again we are drawn back to the autistic core. Buildings are straightforward, straight-edged, their outlines clear. Human beings are . . . nuanced. Architectural perspective-taking is easy. Social perspective-taking is a different matter.

And that was the handicap we were always at work on. Art is important in itself, as autistic obsessions grow beautiful. But for Jessy it has other kinds of importance. It brings her into contact with people. It enhances her communication skills. It gives her a productive way to fill the empty time after work is done. Compared with these advantages, it hardly seems significant that it allows her to make money.

Certainly people buy her paintings, and the checks are no longer nugatory. Clients choose their building; Jessy works as readily from photographs as from her own sketch. (The photos must, however, be sharp and detailed; Jessy can combine, but any attempt at invention will be vague and unconvincing.) Jessy's carefully kept notebook contains seventy-five names and addresses; many of the clients are people she's met. But not all paintings are paid for, and that too is a social lesson, as she works on her gifts for family and friends. A painting is a fine graduation present for a special housemate — she'll make sure that her view of his college dormitory shows his window. And she will provide him a description.

One of the many challenges that confront the family of an autistic person comes when she or he turns twenty-two and school is over. (For the past twenty-five years, federal law has guaranteed education for the handicapped until age twenty-two.) The teachers at Mount Greylock Regional High School had worked with Jessy on reading and writing for nine years. She had achieved what might be called a fourth-grade competence, and we didn't want her to lose it, as she certainly would if it wasn't exercised. So we provided her with factual material on her obsessive interests — books on the planets, brochures, newspaper accounts of power outages — and she read of them what she could. We had her write thank-you letters; *written* politenesses were actually good. Her journals were done at our suggestion. But the descriptions were Valerie's idea, Valerie who had known her so long, and who was still a friend. When Jessy made her a portrait of her bathroom heater, Val suggested she write a description.

The first descriptions were only a couple of sentences, and those heavily prompted. Jessy had no idea how to begin or how to continue. More significant for effective communication, her defective "theory of mind" afforded no insight into what a viewer would find obvious and what he would need to be told. So each description gave not only practice in grammar, syntax, vocabulary, and spelling ("vermilion," "carmine," "cobalt"), but in that fundamental aspect of writing, and living: imagining the reader's point of view. I asked questions: Do you think they'll see the different pinks? How many are there? What do you want to tell them next? And over the years — not months — I was suggesting less and less, and the descriptions got longer and longer. (Several are reproduced in Appendix I.) They became a habit, then an unbreakable routine. Jessy would finish a painting; that night she'd say, "We will write the description."

But one night — seven years later? ten years? I can't keep records of *everything* — I was going out. "We can't write it tonight," I told her, "we'll do it tomorrow." And when I came back it was done. It was a draft, we edited it a bit together, but Jessy had written it. So slow, so gradual, is the building of a simple, essential skill.

· · ·

I have in this chapter already exhibited my own penchant for metaphoric thinking. It's a tempting activity, to read our own meanings into Jessy's pure colors and shapes. "Earth shadow, resembling a rather menacing tornado, hovers behind her sister Katy's house in Cambridge." But the writer of that vivid, and accurate, sentence, knew Jessy well enough to draw back from his suggestion. Describing another painting he makes it clear: "The lightning bolt and the black windowpanes, which contribute to the ominous, almost Gothic quality of this painting, are merely the signs of a power failure for Jessy."[2] When another viewer felt that quality, he remembered Jessy's astronomical interests and speculated about a black hole. But Ernie knew the true source of that intensity. "A blackout, the phenomenon that temporarily disrupts the flow of the appliance world, is cause for great excitement and planning. If rain is in the forecast, Jessy will make sure to set her auxiliary battery-powered alarm clock, lest rain turn to thunderstorm, thunderstorm cause power outage, and power outage stop the clock." Now that *would* be ominous.

In short, Jessy's codes are not ours. Once someone asked for happy colors and Jessy was nonplussed. Once someone thought she should be frightened of the dark. Once someone thought outer weather could symbolize inner weather. But symbols, if they communicate at all, carry socially attributed, agreed-upon meanings. For Jessy, things are what they are, and if they have meanings, they are wholly idiosyncratic. To understand her is to understand that.

. . .

Painting has become part of Jessy's life. It's part of my life too. When she's working on a commission I want to see it every day, not to check up, but to delight in the unfolding process, as color by color, shade by shade, Jessy realizes the order that is already diagrammed in her mind. However odd I find her choices, brilliant or neutral, saturated or pastel, her endgame will, I know, bring them into unpredictable, perfect balance. The work will stretch over months; Jessy takes the long view. Painting is a small part of her full life, an activity like another, just one of the things she does. Certainly she chooses to do it, but I'm by no means sure she'd keep doing it without the continuing reinforcement of checks. When she comes home from work she doesn't rush to her worktable. She'll vacuum first, or relax in her rocker, or take out the trash, or make cookies or tuna fish casserole or Puerto Rican beans; painting is for the bits of afternoons and evenings when she has nothing to do. Except for Saturday nights. Then *Party Mix* is on the radio, and Jessy will put in two hours of concentrated work. It's the only time she listens to music now — it's no longer "too good," but still turned so low that I can barely hear it through her closed door. The Sunday morning viewing is one of my great pleasures.

It's a pleasure for Jessy too. She's pleased to share her painting, to hear me praise the colors, pleased to name them, to tell me the ones she's mixed to produce a particular shade — for she rarely uses a color straight from the tube. Cadmium yellow is hard for her to pronounce, but she'll try, and laugh when she fails with phthalocyanine green and quinacridone rose. She has sixty-two tubes of assorted acrylics, and a new shade is right up there with chocolate as one of the few things she wants to buy. Neatly arranged in spectrum order, her tubes are ready to express her ideal world, organized, certain, fully under her control.

She is pleased to get checks, pleased to have a show, a reception, refreshments. She is pleased to be an artist. Or perhaps "content" is the better adjective. It is her proud parents who are pleased, delighted, thrilled. Jessy is content to be an artist, as she is content to be a mail clerk. After all, to her one activity is no more prestigious than the other.

Yet in art too autism has its hidden land mines, and not only the possibility of a painto. A painto is the worst that can happen when she's alone in her room. But outside, the social world impinges. As she sketches a house, pad in hand, absorbed in penciling in the clapboards that offer opportunities for rainbow upon rainbow, a curious passerby asks a what-question. "What are you making?" That's bad when she's making cookies, bad when she's making art. Jessy knows it may happen; she tries to prepare herself beforehand. Still, she may explode if it catches her unawares. Or at a reception, everything going well — she's enjoying the attention, enjoying the refreshments, enjoying seeing her paintings again (she has no eyes for other people's), enjoying the praise — I make a mistake. Someone tells her she's a wonderful artist. I remind her that a compliment deserves a thank-you, and a happy occasion collapses into misery. We must go outside to recover, leaving the bewildered stranger to wonder what he did wrong. Even here, autism's minuses and pluses are inseparable. But now the pluses last longer.

. . .

When Jessy painted her room last year she used, of course, the full spectrum: violet, blue, green, yellow, orange — and pink, for these are pastels. Not just any pastels, however, but mixed to her specifications. A friend, an architect, brought her four huge volumes of color samples. The whole rainbow was there, hundreds of shades, numbered for a fussy client to choose from. Jessy did not deliberate, she knew; her choice was *instantaneous*. And now her room is not a riot, but a breathtaking harmony of color. Green and orange appear in two shades: mint and lime, pale orange and sunny peach. Each window, each window frame, each door, each door panel, each shelf, each alcove, is a different color. A cupboard faced in tongue-and-groove provides the necessary opportunity to display the full spectrum. This too is art, and Jessy is older now. I think even she would agree that these are happy colors.

PART FOUR

Living

CHAPTER 9 "Because can tell by the face"

It's late; Jessy has been in bed for hours. We are listening to music with friends when she comes down to tell me her radiator is clanking. She's quiet, even polite, but she's annoyed. Her mind is on the sound, the old GAKE of childhood, and she goes straight, not to me, but to another elderly woman, and tells *her*. I recall similar misidentifications; they happen often when former companions come back to see her. But this is the first time it's happened to me. Afterward, when we talk about it, she explains. "Both have white hair."

And that's not even true. Mary's hair is white; mine is a nondescript gray. It's not that Jessy doesn't know the difference between an old friend — she's known Mary for thirty years — and her mother. It's that her mind was full, too full to make the extra effort to attend to the indicators that a normal two-year-old processes so effortlessly that it seems instinctual. And if she can overlook so clear, so visual an indicator as hair color — Jessy, who distinguishes the minutest differences between shades — how can we expect her to pick up the subtle indicators of emotions?

139

And if she can't, how can we expect her to manage the ordinary, inescapable interchanges of living?

. . .

At times we have the eerie feeling that Jessy is a Martian, a visitor from some pure planet where feelings do not exist. (Autistic people have a similar feeling; many of them watch *Star Trek,* and feel, with Temple Grandin, an identification with Mr. Spock.) She asks a question, trying to work it out: "Is it a reason to get sad when old people die?" A friend has called to say he won't be coming to dinner; his father has died suddenly. Well? We had presented the death of grandparents as something to accept without tears — grandfather at eighty-six, confused and depressed, grandmother at ninety-two, incapacitated by a stroke. Jessy believed us. How not? She had picked up no contradictory signals. A normal child would see beneath the apparent acceptance of death to qualify it; our reassurances had unthinkingly assumed that Jessy would recognize our unspoken sadness. Yet we should have known; we knew her cheerful interest in funerals as "a good reason" to miss a day of work and still get paid. It was predictable. "I didn't know people get sad when old people die."

But there is progress. We see a movie. Jessy can follow a film now, if it is simple enough and I am there to provide a running summary; she remembers to this day how the princess in *Star Wars* was sad when the Death Star destroyed her planet. Another movie is about children lost in the Adirondacks. At a moment when they are in grave danger from a murderous tramp who is stalking the little boy with a gun, Jessy surprises me: "I think I am going to cry." Empathy! How long we've waited for it! I tell her they're going to escape, as they fortunately do, and it's all right. Yet two weeks later on a TV western the hero, shot by Indians, has an arrow through his shoulder, obviously a serious wound. A railroad track is visible, however, and a train has been mentioned, so: "He will miss the train?" Or in the cartoon *Pinocchio,* she shows interest in the moon rising, but walks out on the scene of Gepetto and Pinocchio embracing when Pinocchio becomes a real boy. I recall how when she was eighteen a psychologist said she needed to talk about feelings. We tried to provide a vocabulary, only to see her delightedly collect words with similar prefixes — discouraged, disappointed, desperate, depressed, disgruntled, dismayed — her mental energies absorbed in the enterprise of arranging them in hierarchies of severity, her emotions untouched.

Those who live and work with autistic people have many such anecdotes. A woman with an M.A. consoles a friend who's lost her mother; she tells her she knows how she feels because her parakeet has just died. Or there's the teenager reported by Christopher Gillberg, a specialist in autism, who "after the death of his mother, when people asked how he was doing . . . usually answered, 'Oh, I am all right. You see I have Asperger syndrome, which makes me less vulnerable to the loss of loved ones than are most people.'"[1] Everybody dies sometime, I said to Jessy this year apropos of something or other. She replied with her usual cheerfulness. "Then when you die our house will belong to *me!*" And that is perfectly true.

·   ·   ·

How can we expect Jessy to realize that recognizing a friend is more important than worrying about the thermostat setting? It's not more important to *her.* So we tell her. She takes it in, but she isn't a bit upset. Mistakes about people aren't in the same ballpark as putting two socks on the same foot (she cried and made a book about that), or a mistaken box number. It doesn't occur to her that a failure in recognition might hurt someone's feelings. She knows about feeling bad and feeling good. She knows about feeling hurt,

A page from Jessy's journal, considering a
"discouragement."

in your head, your stomach, your foot. But a mental or emotional
hurt — that's a metaphor, that's not so obvious.

What are hurt feelings, anyway? She tells me loudly, "You
hurt my feelings!" Her voice proclaims anger. Or she exclaims,
"My, my feelings are hurt!" This time it's sadness; she's misbe-

haved, and her friend won't take her out to breakfast. Or she asks what she's learned to call a "rhetorical question," as she so often does when she's annoyed at somebody else's mistake. As when her father dropped something on his foot. He said, "Ouch!" loud and sudden, and Jessy, loud and sudden, asked angrily, "Why do you drop it?" But now her father's annoyed; his foot hurts, and this is a question she knows requires no answer. So he says (loud and sudden), "Don't ask me that!" And Jessy notes in her journal, "Discouragement. I am discouraged about hurting my father's feelings." She knows it's a feeling, at least, and she knows it's not about his foot. It's a bad feeling. That's as close as she comes. "Discouragement" is a bad feeling too. Desperate? Disgruntled? Dismayed? Let the d-words go; just call it "sad."

What *is* the right word to use in those social contexts she is increasingly aware of? "Is it an insult when I scream? Is it hurt your feelings?" Or when she has been reproved because she accused a guest at table of stealing her napkin: "'Who stole my napkin?' Is it an insult?" Well, it's almost an insult. It depends on the tone of voice, it depends (I discover as I go along) on the value of the object — "Who stole my money?" is different — *it depends on the context.* "Is it an insult when I say, 'I heard you making that noise?'" "Is it an insult when I say someone died?"

How *do* we learn the right words for these slippery social concepts? Nobody teaches us. Jessy had waited patiently to vacuum the room while her father looked over his slides. He'd said he'd be finished in a minute, but then he looked at some more. Jessy has grown much, much better at waiting, but a good job of patience is hard to extend when you thought it was finished and then it wasn't. She reports to me, "I told my father he lied. Is that an insult?" It's an insult, all right, but is it a lie? Jessy begins her bizarre creaky-door noise, once so familiar, now uncommon —

because she's insulted her father, because she's been corrected, because she's gotten things wrong. She cares about being corrected now, as she didn't in the long, unsocial, indifferent years when she only shrieked about lights and clouds and bells and gongs and the other phenomena of her autistic world. She didn't care then about the niceties of social behavior, or, indeed, whether she could get her shrieking under control, which she does, on this occasion, in less than ten minutes. She really wants to learn, now, to navigate on this mysterious planet of ours, but it's so hard, and it's so hard to help her, and so sad when she fails.

.   .   .

Eric Courchesne writes: "The development of normal social and language skills depends upon the comprehension and use of attention-directing gestures and the coordination of attention among objects and people." In order to comprehend a situation and respond normally within it, the child must be able to detect "salient changes in the environment," stay focused on "channels anticipated to provide relevant information," and effect "smooth, accurate, and rapid shifts of attention in response to attention-directing stimuli such as facial, gestural, and vocal signals during social interactions."[2] If this ability is impaired, the child — and adult — must make do with what we might call "behavioral echolalia," learning behavior as she initially learned speech. Both are learned through imitation; both are delayed in autism; and both are "echoed" exactly, not altered according to the situation. From such rote learning, we should expect strange results. What is relevant information for Jessy may well seem, by non-Martian standards, disconcertingly irrelevant.

So hear Jessy as she mulls over our near accident last week at a dangerous intersection. She was getting a cold that day, or thinks she was — she's very interested in the exact time of onset of colds.

"That means I would have been hurt or killed as well as having a cold." I'm used to it, but even to me this sounds bizarre. It brings back, once again, a day from the long ago, watching my daughter, not yet two, crawling serenely away from us all. "There's nothing the matter with Jessy," I told my neighbor. "She just has a distorted sense of what's important." Words like that are hard to forget.

What's important? What's unimportant? How do we know? How does *she* know, when what's "salient" for her isn't salient for you and me? One Sunday I tell her not to cook me any bacon. Jessy knows why; she knows all about cholesterol. "Because I don't want you to have a stroke." So far, so good — *very* good. But then: "Does it count for taking a personal day?" It does, I assure her. And she thinks it over, working out the rule. "Even if not dead. Just in the family."

She picks up on the news now; that too is progress. When a local girl died in the bombing of Pan Am flight 103, Jessy took in the whole story — the planned Christmas dinner, the empty place, the wrapped presents under the tree — concrete, wrenching details that would be significant to anyone and are significant to Jessy too. She reaches for an appropriate response. "I shall use the big worry doll for grieving." Then she considers; she has smaller worry dolls, and there are hierarchies of grief. "I shall save it for if there is a death in the family." And finally, "But I'm sure it is much worse than if the kitty gone." Who can say she hasn't got it right? Another time the news shows a terribly burned child. We're told it was a nurse's error. Errors, of course, are something she understands. It's harder, though, to work out which of them are important and which unimportant when they're *all* important to her. "This is an error that I [ought to] get upset. Never mind that typo on the computer!"

Over the years I've come to understand these episodes better. Of course she knows about important and unimportant; we've been working on that since she was able — at fifteen, maybe — to understand the words. She knows, too, that she isn't sure which is which. So, with that busy mind of hers, so good at inferring the rules of numbers, at systematizing hierarchies, she's trying to work out *these* rules. She reviews them again and again, trying to get them clear. There are rules for work — there are (a new word) *priorities*. There are priorities at home, priorities everywhere. They may not be Jessy's own. They rarely are. But she has learned to accept them, if we give her time, if we take her through them gradually, step by step. It's a process of negotiation, between us and her, between family needs and her own desires, between herself and the world. I've given striking examples, odd enough even to seem funny. Mostly, though, it's a matter not of weird contrasts but of ordinary, everyday living.

As when, unexpectedly, we can't go for our regular Saturday shopping. Daddy needs the car to visit his stepmother, a shut-in he hasn't seen for months. Jessy, of course, is distressed, though now, mostly, she can control herself. This time there are no tears or screams, only the familiar, insistent questioning. If we can't go to the supermarket, if we can't get all the things on the list, what will happen?

I walk her through it. We do need a great many things, but we can get them at the downtown market. It becomes clear, however, that the particular items that Jessy has in mind, Stella D'oro cookies and Orville Redenbacher popcorn, are not available downtown. Considerable talk, then, about this, as I present the possibilities: we can do without cookies, we can do without popcorn, we can buy another brand. Jessy acknowledges these alternatives, which she knows well enough. Reluctantly, repetitively, she acquiesces. *But that is not the end of the process.* Finally, she repeats to herself (in question form, but she knows the answer) the correct priorities: "Is it more important to go see Winifred

The Great Stained Glass Doors in Spring at Dawn, #10, 5/1/89.

*St. Paul's and St. Andrew's Methodist Church and the Migraine Type
Lightning and the Elves,* 10/17/98.

George Washington Bridge with the Light Pillar Reflections, 2/1/99.

The Flatiron Building with the Rosy Light and the Pinkish Lightning,
9/26/99.

than to get popcorn and Stella D'oro?" I have, of course, spent the last half hour telling her exactly that, that Winifred is lonely, that she hasn't seen Daddy for months. Though her question is "rhetorical," I answer, "Yes." And Jessy is now ready to affirm the principle no normal seven-year-old needs to have made explicit: It is more important to go see a shut-in relative than to get popcorn.

. . .

Jessy was nearing twenty when one of the young companions set her a new goal. Taking a sheet of paper, Joann wrote at the head of it, THINKING OF OTHERS. She helped Jessy think of a few things that might consist of. They listed them. The formal layout helped focus Jessy's attention; the examples gave the social abstraction specific, concrete meanings. Jessy has spent the ensuing twenty years extending those meanings into something that may be called a general concept.

At first it was a behavioral category, its instances specified and rewarded. Then, as Jessy got the idea, she began to come up with her own examples. Not that she had miraculously acquired insight into other people's feelings; you still had to — still have to — *tell* her you are sad, and her ritualized "I hope you will feel better" is not really very comforting. Thinking of Others remained touchingly concrete: "I put nutmeg instead of cinnamon in the pudding because I know you don't like that." She told us she didn't need us to make an Easter egg hunt for her anymore — but she made one for us. When two good friends came to visit she put two lollipops and two Nabisco wafers by their bed, bought with her own money. She even began to connect her own experience with other people's; remembering when she lost her wallet, she could reflect, "If I find a wallet with identification I will call that number and 'I found a wallet' and that person will be so *relieved!*" The situation was hypothetical, but the attribution of feelings, even the adjective, was correct.

Thinking of others, of course, is hard when you don't have a "theory of mind" to allow you to see something from another point of view. Even in the unemotional, physical world, Jessy can't do this. She locks the door behind her when she leaves for work, even though she knows I'm still inside and there's no need to. She scrapes the ice off the windshield on the passenger's side, her side, leaving the driver's side obscured. She thinks I can see what she sees; if she knows something, she thinks the person she's talking to knows it too. We are back in chapter 3, with the Sally-Anne test. For years we wondered; now we know that in autism it is the cognitive, not the emotional, handicap that is primary.

Nevertheless, in social life it is the emotional that is salient. It is that handicap, that lack, that we notice first, that troubles us most as we try to communicate to our autistic child, as we did to our other children, that extraordinary triumph of thought and feeling we call the Golden Rule. "How would *you* feel," we asked them, if Tommy hit *you*, grabbed *your* cookie, told *you* he hated you? Clever George Bernard Shaw said not to do unto others as you would have them do unto you because tastes differ. But even that iconoclastic reversal recognizes the rule's emotional core, as the fact that we call it a rule recognizes its cognitive, generalizable element. But by whatever combination of rational and emotive we ourselves understand — and feel — it best, whether we elevate it to a religious principle or reduce it to simple good manners, whether we honor it in the breach or not at all, it is the foundation of civilized social life.

Jessy was late into her teens before it made any sense to try her on "How would you feel if." And even then her own translation reveals what she made of it: "Tit for tat."

It was my own failure of imagination. Of course I'd learned that I couldn't rely on words alone to reach Jessy's understanding; I had to illustrate any new idea through action. Unfortunately it is far easier to illustrate Socrates' negative formulation of the rule than Jesus' positive one. I do something nice for you. It feels good. That's how people feel when you do something nice for them. You want them to feel good, don't you? Even to me it doesn't sound compelling. The Socratic version is more immediate: Don't do unto others as you wouldn't have them do unto you. Maybe Tommy did hit you, but don't hit him back.

But with no convenient Tommy at hand, the best I could think of was, I fear, the worst. There were plenty of things Jessy did unto others that she wouldn't like done to her. She snapped. She hit — not hard, but she did. She even came at one good friend with a rake. All I could think of was to do the same thing to her, as far as possible in exactly the same way. Jessy didn't like loud, sudden noises. She certainly didn't like being hit. Nobody had ever come after her with a rake, but if they had, she might have been frightened but her feelings wouldn't have been hurt. Socrates' rule brought her no nearer to understanding why her friend Tracy never came back. It's not surprising she made it into tit for tat, and experienced it not as teaching but as punishment. Only the capacity to imagine other people's feelings can distinguish tit for tat from the Golden Rule, the Old Law from the New. And it's not enough to imagine them; you have to put them before your own. That's hard enough for normal human beings.

Nevertheless, slowly, slowly, it begins to happen, even for Jessy, even through tit for tat. "Why aren't you unpacking the groceries?" Jessy asks angrily. "Why aren't you helping in the garden?" I reply, and she understands. Or we arrange to feed her brother's cats for four days: he will come stay with her when we go away. You help me, I help you, is fair exchange. How many people never get any farther?

But Jessy is going farther. Now she spontaneously verbalizes the principle Joann taught her half her life ago. Someone gives her a book about insects. It has a scorpion on the cover, and Jessy is interested in the story I tell her, that when her brother was a baby in Ceylon a scorpion almost bit him but we killed it. Her busy mind works it over. "So if a scorpion had bit him, then would have no brother." Pause. "And that's a good reason to cry even if it [makes you] exposed to cold." And then, astonishingly, "Because it's better to feel sick than selfish."

It's a highly hypothetical outcome for a healthy brother in his midforties. I'm even more joyful when principle leads to action. Last year she put the cat's water bowl outside the bathroom when she took her shower. It wasn't pure altruism, for she did not want to hear Daisy scratching at the door. Still, by her lights she had earned the right to say, as she did, "That is thinking of others." But *this* year — I was already working on this book — she thought, not of Daisy's comfort, but really, truly, genuinely, of her father's.

We were walking together on the beach. It was windy and cold, and she decided to go up to the house for a sweatshirt. She came back wearing it, but there was something else over her arm. Her father's jacket! Forty years of growing! It was worth the wait.

. . .

Charity begins at home, but there is more to thinking of others than thinking of your own family. Very early we provided a jar in the kitchen "for the poor children," and Jessy contributed her penny too. Poor children had no nice house, no good food, no Christmas tree. She must have taken some of that in, because it was many years before she could verbalize "others" that she made her book about the poor Indian family. But it was not until recently that her enthusiasm for weather phenomena propelled her beyond such unrealized generalities.

For days the big news on the Weather Channel was Hurricane Mitch. Jessy followed its course with interest; hurricanes can be classified, their changing strengths expressed in numbers. TV showed her Mitch's results: mud slides and devastation in countries she'd never heard of, Nicaragua, Honduras. I marked the newspaper reports for her and she read them. "Honduras is one of the poorest countries in the Western Hemisphere." "Over 6000 people died. Over a million lost their homes. Over 10,000 were injured and over 5000 disappeared. Over 80 bridges were destroyed and countless roads are impassable." We went through our closets. Willingly Jessy took the bags to the collection point; spontaneously she applied her phrase, "That is thinking of others." At the benefit carol service, she was enthusiastic as she put her own five-dollar bill in the basket. She even used the word "charity," which I didn't know she knew. (Still, she suggested next day that the people in Honduras could "evacuate," take a plane, a ship, to somewhere else, and had to be reminded they were too poor.)

There is personal altruism, and there is citizenship. Though I've worked hard on one, I've held back on the other. So I was surprised this year when amid vague talk concerning the next election Jessy informed me that the president can't have a third term and that President Roosevelt had almost four. When on earth did she learn that? Then I remembered Marilyn, one of the most inspired of the Jessy-companions, tireless in thinking up activities Jessy could enjoy and interactions that could extend her social behavior. Marilyn must have told her. Jessy was already twenty-two when Marilyn lived with us. Ronald Reagan was running for president, and Marilyn thought Jessy should register to vote.

We didn't think so. Much as we thought the country could use another vote against Reagan, it didn't seem right it should come from Jessy, who barely knew he was alive and had no idea what he or any other president might do. Jessy remained unregistered.

Fast forward. We're in the kitchen glued to the television, listening to the three-way debates of 1992, when suddenly Jessy pipes up, "You're talking about the deficit!" Already interested in bank statements, she knew about deficits, and she didn't like them. We'd also been talking about store closings; her sister had closed one of her shops, because of something called a recession. I showed her a report of another Main Street store closing — something to read, something to expand awareness. I certainly wasn't prepared for Jessy's question: "Is it because of Bush?"

I attempt to explain that many factors go into a store closing, that it's not the fault of just one person, even the president. But Jessy needs clear, definite answers; she's already lost interest. Yet not altogether. Next day the local paper continues the story. "Guess what! I read that about Newberry's and it *is* because of Bush!"

Shift forward again. It's 1999, and there's not a deficit but a surplus. Jessy hasn't noticed; she doesn't know that word. Shall I tell her about it? She'd have no doubt whom to vote for. After so many years, is it time for Marilyn's efforts to bear fruit?

I don't know. Parents have their limits, and not just from aging. As her father couldn't take her as far in math as she could go, so I don't know if I can, if I want to, if I *should,* propel Jessy into a citizen's responsibility. Yes, she pays taxes, the concrete sign of it, and she understands at least some of the things that taxes go for. But can I take her to register, knowing her interest rides on the simplicity of an obsession — worse, that her vote would be no true choice but a mere echo of what we told her? Yet there are other single-issue voters, after all, and this issue is preferable to many I can think of. I don't know. I just don't know.

. . .

But I do know there's progress, that Jessy's still growing. That she's not merely, passively, being taught, but taking in hand her own journey toward empathy, thinking about it, *working* at it. Now, as I write, she is reviewing, confirming her social rules. Should she refuse when she's asked to work overtime? "Only if I have another appointment, like giving blood. Because thinking of others is *important*." To think of others you have to notice how they feel. "I will learn by the voice when someone is irritated. Loud." Four days later: "I will remember how people feel when they get irritated. First the voice is loud and abrupt. But expression could be wrinkle face. Like frowning."

"Sometimes can tell when people are happy even if not smiling because can tell by the face. When people are happy eyes always glow and face shine like sun. And if people are sad face always looks gloomy like clouds. And between happy and sad like partly cloudy." Jessy said that twenty years ago, and joyfully I wrote it down. But did she say it or *know* it? Years went by and I heard nothing like it again. Maybe Joann told her that; maybe she only picked up on it because of sun and clouds. But now it's spontaneous, now she's noticing, now she's *focusing* on those subtle indicators. Now she's beginning to understand. When her load of magazines and catalogs breaks the janitor's recycling bag, on her own she goes and gets him a new one. And she tells me, "I felt so bad for that janitor!" Let the millennium begin.

CHAPTER 10 "I guess Darth Vader learned from consequences! Like me!"

Inside the kitchen folder there is, not an envelope — an envelope's not big enough — but another folder. It's full and it grows fuller. It's labeled Social. Its bulk is a reminder of what we slowly realized: that after the years of easy teaching, years of discovering the possibilities of what Jessy could learn, even excel at, there remained the wide expanse of things she could never excel at, that she could learn only partially and with the greatest difficulty.

Not that the teaching I now call easy ever felt easy. It was years before I got Jessy to feed herself; more years before she used the toilet. Even skills she had mastered, like climbing stairs, or marking with a crayon, or putting together a puzzle, would be lost and have to be introduced again. Teaching and maintaining the ordinary skills of childhood was a continual attempt to coax, to lure her past Kanner's "obsessive desire for the maintenance of sameness" — past the barriers raised by her desire to continue what she was already doing, her contentment in remaining just where she was. Far more often than not the attempt was fruitless. I

154

collected inspirational maxims to help me through the days — Nietzsche's "What doesn't kill me makes me stronger," or, after an especially hard week, the words of the Dutch liberator William the Silent: "It is not necessary to hope in order to undertake; it is not necessary to succeed in order to persevere."

In the midst of these years of mingled frustration and tedium, it's not surprising that the few areas of Jessy's clear, quick excellence took on a special importance. We used to say that the world was divided into things you couldn't teach Jessy and things you didn't have to teach her. That, of course, was an exaggeration. It might take eight years before she dressed herself completely, but eventually she did. Still, the contrast was striking between the things you must walk her through step by step, over and over, and the things you did not so much teach as *show*. Colors, shapes, letters (those too are shapes), numbers, later the system of musical notation — for such things her learning was so immediate it seemed we had merely drawn her attention to what she had always known. It was natural, then, that such achievements became for us lights shining in darkness — or, less melodramatically, signals, glimpsed through uncertain and shifting clouds. Peacock green and peacock blue, heptagons and dodecagons, factors and functions, were not merely welcome, they were thrilling. If Jessy couldn't read — and at the height of her mathematical obsession she could read only three or four words together — if she couldn't follow a story, we had these to hold on to, to marvel at and enjoy.

We had been glad when the psychologist told us our three-year-old had no intellectual deficiency. We — and the psychologist — should have known. Jessy was brilliant at the form-board, but that was *all* she could do. She couldn't identify common objects, even by pointing. She couldn't follow the simplest verbal directions. She could find nothing to do with the doll family. Silently, accurately, the testing recorded what we would fully comprehend only later: that it was in the ordinary world of human living and human relationships that the hardest work was to come. Inside the folder marked Social, spilling out of it into the suitcase, are the records of that work, continual and continuing, on the necessary conditions of life outside Nirvana. It was, and is, the most important work of all.

Intellectual achievement is useless without social development. My grandmother knew this. Long before Jessy was even thought of she used to say to me (to my intense irritation), "Be good, sweet child, and let who will be clever." But we are a clever family, and it's natural that we should value intellectual achievement, natural too that in years when there was little to rejoice at we rejoiced in Jessy's primes. But one cannot live in a world of prime numbers. It helped put things in proportion when we met, as we sometimes did, other autistic young people who were intellectually far more advanced than Jessy, but whose demeanor and behavior made it unlikely that anyone would care to spend much time with them. Unquestionably Jessy has intellectual capacities that have not been developed. She might have learned to work with computers. She might have learned calculus. She might have learned mathematical processes of which I know only the names. Yet though I regret possibilities left unpursued, I do not regret that instead of mathematics Jessy's energies, and ours, have gone into the development of as attractive a human being as the circumstances allowed.

.   .   .

Until Jessy was in her teens, all our teaching had been what is now called "incidental." We had no set plan, no list of goals. We searched the environment for learning opportunities and took them as they arose. We latched onto her interests — which meant her obsessions — and did what we could with them. Knowing her as we did, we could nudge, even push, and draw back as we approached her level of tolerance, abandoning that particular area of learning to another day, another year. It was a regime that minimized frustration or failure, and it was reasonably successful.

But to the degree that it was successful, it could not last. The more Jessy entered the world, the more she was exposed to the unpredictabilities and uncertainties that were so hard for her to tolerate. New experiences poured in upon her, bringing new opportunities but also new demands. And for a long time it was the demands, not the opportunities, that were experienced most acutely.

It is in the nature of learning and growing that as more is mastered, more is expected. Jessy now had to try to do many more things she didn't like or that she couldn't do or did badly. Now not only we, but she herself, experienced failure and frustration, in the bus, in the classroom, in the supermarket, in the street. Because less is forgiven a teenager than a child, she had to work harder than ever before on the do's and don'ts of social behavior. She couldn't scream in the school bus (but she did). She couldn't push the teacher against the wall (but she did). She couldn't smell people, or go up to them and touch their clothes. She couldn't cut into the cafeteria line. She couldn't scream when she typed a period for a comma, or bite her hand. The list of don'ts of social living is endless. So is the list of do's.

It was at this point in Jessy's life that we encountered the little mechanism that was to make such a difference, to bring so much, so fast, within her list of capabilities. She was just fourteen.

It was a golf counter. Golfers wear it on their wrists to keep score. Jessy had seen one on another child, much less severely autistic, who had come to visit. It was everything she liked: it was mechanical, it was easy to use, it was predictable, it was numerical, it clicked. Her birthday was coming up and *she wanted one* — the first present besides candy she'd ever asked for. So it was under the best possible circumstances that we began our homemade program in behavior modification.

Behavior modification is not an attractive term, and the term "operant conditioning" is worse. Who wants to believe that learning is a matter of conditioning, of rewards and penalties, that what worked for B. F. Skinner's pigeons will work for her child? We knew about behavior modification; we'd heard Ivar Lovaas speak at autism conventions. We were impressed with his pioneering work with autistic children, but we were also complacent. We'd already managed to teach toileting and self-help skills; we'd come a long way with language. Did we need this? Did Jessy?

But Jessy wanted that counter. We followed her lead, and she led us, all unknowing, as close as we've ever come to that thing so often claimed, so seldom found, a breakthrough.

The program had two elements: points for desirable behaviors (leading, if the number agreed on was reached, to a Popsicle at the end of the day), and a written contract.[1] It was important, I think, that Jessy was involved in both, that the process was not entirely imposed from without. It was Jessy who awarded the points, or subtracted them for such behaviors as hitting and screaming, whether or not I was present. Sometimes she made her own bar graph of the week's numbers, in coordinated colors (lemonlemonlemon lime!). The day she reached 145½ when the goal was only 100, I realized that for mathematical Jessy not the Popsicle but the points themselves were her reward. The Popsicles were dropped unnoticed.

Even more important, Jessy and I negotiated the contract together. Shared attention! We made of our Sunday contract sessions a social occasion, both actually, as we sat side by side on her bed and reviewed the successes and failures of the past week, and theoretically, as I took the opportunity to talk about people's behavior in general. Her enjoyment was obvious; much as she resisted reading, she loved reading the contracts, which I kept easily within her own vocabulary and comprehension.

One day, after more than a year of this, I set a long-term goal. I had taught Jessy to swim in the usual way, without points, but she would still not go out of her depth or swim more than the two or three feet necessary to reach my outstretched arms. If we contracted for 1000 points for swimming the length of the pool, I thought, we'd have something to work up to during the next year. What happened? That very night she walked up to the deep end of the pool, jumped in, and swam the 75-foot length *eight times*.

Another incident, though less spectacular, had greater significance for social development. At this time, though Jessy was friendly, even affectionate with people she knew well, we had been unable to persuade her to make the simplest greeting: no hello, no smile, no looking in the eye. On the contract, then, went "Hello" (1 point). Plus a proper name: "Hello, Mrs. Smith" (2 points). Plus eye contact (3 points). Plus a fourth point for doing it all "spontaneously"; in Jessy's words, "without told." Suddenly we began to get reports from school; from Mrs. Smith and Mrs. Jones and the speech therapist whose father was a London psychoanalyst and who had been working with Jessy for more than a year. "Hello, Mrs. Smith." The click-click-click-click was hardly noticeable. And the new greetings, of course, elicited smiles and delight; Mrs. Smith and Mrs. Jones did not have to be programmed to deliver social reinforcement. Jessy was learning far more than mechanical greeting behavior. She was learning something even more foreign to her — to enjoy approval, since points and approval went together. If Jessy can now say, "I'm proud of myself," and mean it; if she can repeat, "If at first you don't succeed, try, try again," and understand it, it is the result not of deep therapy that penetrated fourteen years of autistic refusal, but of clear behavioral specifications and that little counter.

. . .

Autistic refusal. It had been with her from the beginning, that hidden, withheld quality of so much she did and didn't do, so that again and again we had to lure, almost trick, her into performing even activities that were clearly within her capabilities; so that again and again "couldn't" and "wouldn't" seemed indistinguishable. I had thought of that inertia as autism's core, its deepest, most fundamental, most massive handicap.

I could scarcely believe, then, how shallow were its roots. The counter opened up an alternative explanation, less poetic than an existential refusal but closer to the facts of our experience. The contract worked because it showed Jessy exactly what to do and gave her a reason for doing it. The counter worked, with this child who counted before she could talk, for whom numbers possessed mysterious significance, because it provided for the first time a truly significant reward for effort. The tasks of development are hard; hard enough for normal children, harder for Jessy. She had not only to acquire ordinary self-help skills, but to surmount her communication handicap, to attend to speech and practice it, and to control her bizarre anxieties and the bizarre behavior that accompanied them. Why should she try to do these things? What motivates a child to grow?

Why even ask the question? Growth is "natural," a child "develops," its potentialities "unfold." The words themselves, in their root meanings, proclaim inevitability. We think about the process only when it fails to occur. But consider the child born to autism, able to understand unvarying shapes, routines, rules, but lacking the ability to interpret the constantly shifting, interlocking, mutually dependent appearances that make up the contexts in which human beings carry on their lives. Such a child will have no *reason* to master those hard developmental tasks. The normal child has strong social reasons to undertake them, to use the toilet like Daddy, to tie its shoes like Katy, to say words, elicit smiles, hugs, approval. Praise encourages it to do what comes naturally even to our cousins the apes, to imitate and join the life around it, to grow independent, to grow up. Children want to be like other people, and when they fail they are embarrassed or ashamed. But Jessy had no idea what it was to be like other people; she was as immune to embarrassment as she was to emulation. Praise had been meaningless to her; it came at her out of the inexplicable universe of what other people think and want. When praised she had tuned out, or worse, stopped the behavior that elicited it. Now, in her fifteenth year, it began to take on meaning — as a side effect of abstract numbers, of the mechanical reinforcement of a golf counter.

One Friday, after a year and a half of contracts, Jessy's teacher called; she had something important to tell me. "Jessy and I have made a decision. Jessy's not going to work for points anymore, she's going to work for praise." And Jessy echoed, "Work for praise!" I was surprised at the suddenness of this unilateral decision, yet I understood it. The school had had nothing to do with administering the contract; Jessy had credited and debited herself, with the autistic, rule-bound exactitude that knows no possibility of cheating. But with her astonishing penchant for categorization, she had subdivided her list of behaviors, originally consisting of a few simple items, into a proliferating complexity of subitems, and true to form was now in danger of occupying herself more with counting clicks than with the behaviors themselves. I had tried to "fade the prompts," to reduce the number of items — they now covered two full pages — but the system was Jessy's, and it had taken on an autistic life of its own. Now I was told that Jessy and the teacher had decided to go cold turkey — no points, no contract. I didn't think it would work; I anticipated a hellish weekend and a return to contract security, but I always support the teacher, and I said, "Fine."

But it did work. All the behaviors were maintained. Jessy kept on setting the table, taking out the trash, washing her underwear — all the simple, concrete acts that the contract had first rendered possible, then automatic. And of course with every one, we praised. We smiled, we hugged, we said, "Jessy, that's good, that's wonderful!" And after each instance Jessy, now smiling in open pleasure, chirped, "Is this praise? Is this praise?" The counter had taught her to enjoy praise, she had agreed to work for it, and *she didn't even know the meaning of the word*. Mathematical abstractions might be obvious, but not this kind of abstraction — social, relational, taking all its meaning from human interaction. I recalled an earlier lesson the contract had taught not her but me: that Jessy had no idea what I meant when I included such items as Saying Something Interesting or Doing Something to Help. I'd learned to specify, say, six helpful behaviors, to define subjects of conversation that might conceivably be considered interesting. From those specifics Jessy could begin to grasp the social generalization, even, over the years, recognize new examples of the simple social category that practice had rendered familiar.

. . .

Behavior modification worked miraculously at the swimming pool, when there was no real resistance and only motivation was lacking. It worked miraculously with concrete actions that Jessy could understand, that she could do easily if she would. Doing

Something to Help, for example, brought in a host of new activities. Jessy, it turned out, was perfectly willing to wash, to iron, to vacuum the whole house, and soon did it "without told." For things like these, the word "breakthrough" was entirely appropriate, and the gains were both permanent and significant. Every new occupation, after all, was an alternative to her sterile fallback activities, to sifting silly business or rocking.

In addressing the handicaps of autism, however, no breakthroughs occurred. As the months passed and behaviors like Hitting and Screaming and Touching People's Clothes remained on the contract, or more discouraging still, were dropped only to reappear weeks later, it became clear that behavior modification was a method, not a magic bullet, a method whose limitations were as significant as its powers. It was too much to imagine that complex social concepts could be built up piecemeal from a collection of imperfectly understood examples. Jessy was enthusiastic about doing a Big Job, Medium Job, or Little Job for a graded number of points. She could even understand how these translated into Something to Help. Doing Something Nice for Somebody, however, was not so accessible. It wasn't easy to make niceness specific, considering how much individuals and circumstances differ. In social experience, we concluded, the contract could at most begin a process. The writing, the reading, the explanations, the repetitions, could introduce an idea and reinforce it. That was hardly miraculous, but it was worth doing. Though behavior modification couldn't teach sensitive, imaginative, individualized moral responses, though Thinking of Others was years down the road, focusing on the possibilities of Doing Something Nice was a step forward.

Similarly, points and contracts only made a beginning in modifying autistic behaviors. Yet those behaviors were the greatest obstacles in her social habilitation. These were the things that disconcerted people, annoyed them, upset and bewildered them, frightened them, even on occasion disgusted them. Mumbling, rocking, making faces. Hitting, of course. Screaming. Crying. And the myriad instances of social unconsciousness: how could they be distinguished from deliberate rudeness? So Jessy must learn to notice things she had never noticed. She must try not to push aside people in her way; try not to walk between people who were talking to each other; try not to walk away when people were talking to *her*. These were the behaviors that brought many penalties and few rewards.

We had held off introducing negative points for the first two months of contracts, until our warm Sunday routines had become habitual. Jessy didn't like making her first subtractions, but among all the positives she soon got used to them. It was always possible to redeem a lapse by a Big Job, or using tenses correctly (we had put grammar in the contract), or diving from the side of the pool. Nor was it especially hard for her to control her more innocuous misbehaviors — those that bespoke not so much autism itself as immaturity and developmental delay. She could stop staring at dog feces if she got points for doing so. She could manage not to talk about people's illnesses or handicaps; a penalty for mentioning the art teacher's diabetes in front of him never had to be imposed. But points had much less power over the world within. The behaviors related to her obsessions and compulsions were much more difficult for her to control. Yet these were the most disconcerting, the most unpredictable, the most bewildering of all.

She cried when her superball didn't reach the seventh bounce. She cried when someone took her special seat (only she knew what made it special) on the school bus. She cried about "forgetting to look" at a particular billboard on her route. She cried about politenesses. She cried when somebody had a cold. She cried when *she* had a cold. And how she cried!

Much later, after she'd seen *Rain Man,* Jessy would call these hypersensitivities her "autisms."* We called them her "allergies." The word was more than a metaphor; her responses were as instant, as involuntary, as any allergic reaction. "Wee-alo, wee-alo," she'd cry, "la, la," her face distorted, her heart pounding, every muscle in her body tensed, her mouth open so wide we could see the flattened tongue within. Desolating for her, terrifying for the stranger, such extreme reactions overwhelmingly suggested a neurological base. So too with the positive reactions, with the shivering, unbearable intensity with which she experienced the too-good. She didn't cry about too-good names and numbers and special words. But she wouldn't say them, and lest she should hear them she covered her ears, smiling her secret smile. Harmless as that might seem at home, even, in moderation, charming, it was destructive of the focused attention necessary for school tasks. When Jessy was in Nirvana, she wasn't learning.

Yet even over autistic behaviors the contract had some power. At the very least it made her conscious of what had been wholly unconscious. On one contract — it was the eighteenth month — I wrote down Jessy's own triumphant words for her to savor: "This is the first time I didn't mumble for whole week!" Though she mumbled the next week and many times thereafter, that was all right. Rome wasn't built in a day.

---

*Hypersensitivities, of course, are characteristic of autism. But these tend to be straightforwardly physical — intolerance of certain sounds, for instance, or textures. Jessy is reasonably comfortable in the physical world; she seems indifferent to extremes of heat or cold, for all her interest in the Weather Channel. Her sensitivities are not of the body but of the mind.

. . .

Jessy's "allergies" would have been unendurable for her and all around her if they had lasted. But though the pain was acute, it was transitory; when it was over it was *over*. An hour later she would be eager to talk about the behavior, the circumstances, the penalty, not merely without resentment but with enthusiasm. "I threw a scene in school. And I made a scream and a cry for two and a half hours. And I mumbled. And bang a chair and I broke a chair. And I bang the door! Crying for a long time is *serious* because it makes people so nervous they have to leave!" Jessy was full of smiles as she told me this. The contrast between the original distress and the subsequent cheerfulness was so striking that we began to think about how social unconsciousness could reduce the power of pain.

So much of our pain is rooted in the responses of other people, or rather, in our perceptions of what those responses are or (even more painful) what they may be. Will people hate me? Not invite me to their party? Will they think I'm babyish? Worst of all, will they laugh at me? Jessy had many anxieties, but these were not among them. Autism was named from the Greek word for "self," and self-involvement has its advantages. The common description for an autistic child is "seems to be in a world of his own." Jessy was the center of her universe; now her own behavior had become not only a focus of attention, but a rich source of interest. We felt for Jessy when she cried and cried. We certainly felt for her teachers and helpers; we knew that for what Jessy put them through, "nervous" was a mild word, and that they did not recover from the experience as quickly as she did. Still, smiles followed tears; they kept working and Jessy kept trying, and together they moved forward.

. . .

Mingling pain and pleasure, contract and points, made possible the slow, partial, yet significant social gains of Jessy's adolescence, while the social unawareness that rewards and penalties could scarcely touch preserved her from what would otherwise have been a continual series of assaults on her self-esteem. Children can be cruel in the face of the abnormal, but Jessy paid no attention to the names they called her. It was her friends from the art room who felt the hostility, not only that directed at Jessy — which, confronted with her indifference, soon stopped — but that which was deflected to them.

Anna and Diana had become the special ed teacher's assistants, and they paid a price. They were followed into the girls' room, peeked at in the stalls, called whores who loved mentals. And here I must pay another of the tributes that are integral to this story. For of all us amateur behavior therapists, Anna and Diana were the bravest and the toughest and the most successful. I didn't see what they did at school; I heard of the ugly names only much later. But for two summers they lived with us, and I still marvel at what they accomplished. In fact as I return to the notes I wrote then, I wonder if I haven't undersold the power of behavior modification. It may well be that the limitations I have just attributed to the method, or to the intractability of autism, were in fact my own. For with counter and contract and humor and affection and teenage resilience, Anna and Diana took on autistic behaviors — not all of them but a lot of them — and triumphed. By the end of the first summer, Jessy, with points for Trying a New Food, was eating almost everything. She was no longer insisting that our salads contain only four stereotyped ingredients or that her food be served on her octagonal plate. As a bonus, that was the summer the twins set her to portraiture — for a reward, of course.

Anna and Diana were much better than I was at thinking up rewards. Points were delightful when there were enough of them, but so were visits to the ice-cream parlor and the shopping trips Jessy loved and I hated. So was *fun* — fun that comes so much easier to teenagers than to a fifty-year-old mother. Watching the twins with Jessy, seeing that they really liked being with her, I realized once more what we are so ready to forget under stress, the supreme importance of gaiety and laughter. There is no more useful tool in living with autism than a kind of rollicking high spirits. "Assume a virtue if you have it not," Hamlet told his mother. If you don't feel like laughing, ham it up anyway. Laugh and the world laughs with you. To add glumness to disability is to double its crippling power. Jessy's cheeriness still smooths her way.

But the summer wasn't all fun. Anna and Diana were also more steadfast in imposing penalties than I had been. Any account of our experience of behavior modification would be incomplete without Jessy's hellos — not the automatic greeting she learned to make, but something very different. The hellos were so ingrained, so long established, that I had resigned myself to the idea that we, and Jessy, would have to live with them for the rest of our lives.

For some years Jessy had suffered from a devastating verbal tic. At the end of every sentence — *every* sentence, sometimes every phrase — came an automatic, meaningless "hello," often trailed by proliferating syllables that made her speech even harder to understand than it was already. I'd tried everything, I thought — coaxing, withholding favorite foods until they were properly asked for, positive and negative points. Nothing worked. The behavior, I decided, was simply not within Jessy's powers of control.

That summer, with Anna and Diana on board and Jessy's brother to support them, Jessy's father and I were able to go on a trip. When we came back the hellos were gone.

They had been extinguished by the very methods I had given up on, applied with the severity I hadn't been able to muster. A hundred negative points for each hello, hello. Add them up hello, two hundred hello, three hundred in a minute hello, thousands in an hour. Of course Jessy had screamed and wailed and shrieked. The teenage therapists waited it out. They told us how long the miracle had taken: four terrible, successful hours.

The steadfast deductions were an essential ingredient in the mix that liberated Jessy. But they were not the only ingredient. Without the atmosphere of affection and mutuality the twins had created, I doubt any such miracle would have taken place. The twins did everything with Jessy. They swam with her, mowed the grass with her, hung up the laundry with her, and they did it all because they wanted to. She was their project and their pleasure; I could never have *asked* anyone to spend as much time with her as they did. They even extended mutuality to points; to Jessy's contract for July 28, 1973, are appended contracts for Anna, Diana, and Paul, *in Jessy's own handwriting*. Anna, like Jessy, got points for Trying New Foods; Diana lost them for Failing to Exercise; big brother penalized himself for Bad Words and Not Writing One Translation of a French Sonnet Every Week. Jessy's counter got a workout, and everybody had fun. I'll never know how much I could have accomplished if my love had been as tough as theirs, for you haven't read this far without realizing that (though the hellos never came back) many of the problem behaviors are still with us. But to this day Jessy won't snap at Anna as she will at the rest of us. "Anna is *strict!*" she says cheerfully when I ask her why.

It was, however, another fifteen years before we came across a method that addressed directly the physical intensities that accompanied Jessy's hypersensitivities. I met June Groden at one of those meetings of the Autism Society of America where assembled parents and professionals learn so much from one another. June knew autism, and she had been working with behavior therapy for many years. I told her about the obsessiveness, the hyperreactivity, the compulsiveness that still resisted Jessy's efforts and ours. She suggested that Jessy, the contracts long behind her, might be interested in trying something new: "imagery scenes." So Jessy, nearly thirty, embarked on a second therapeutic journey.

What June had developed, in her school for autistic and brain-damaged children, was individualized scenarios designed to enable a person — he or she need not be autistic — to deal with the particular stressful situations that were causing trouble. The method is related to what is called in the trade "desensitization," in which phobic patients are gradually accustomed to confronting and conquering their crippling fears. The twins had used it before they knew its name, when with rewards and jokes and fun and persistence they had got Jessy to tolerate some too-good music. The Groden method also used rewards. But to desensitization it added relaxation.

Relaxation, however, went far beyond soothing backrubs and useless exhortations not to be tense. It was a technique, to be taught and practiced. Like the contracts, it was specific, prescriptive, repetitive — exactly the kind of thing Jessy liked and could understand. And she could read about it in a book.[2]

Imagery scenes differed from conventional desensitization in another respect. Phobic patients confront their fears in actual situations. With imagery scenes the process, from original stressor to final reward, takes place entirely in imagination — *except* for the relaxation. That is real.

June presented the whole thing to Jessy as an actual prescription, to be taken three times a day. It consisted of a series of five or six index cards. Typical is the scenario "Someone criticizes me at work." That's the first card. Then, "I get upset but I say STOP [Jessy has drawn a stop sign], RELAX [written in wavy capitals]." Next card: "I say to myself, 'Everybody makes mistakes. No big deal.'" Next, "I feel proud that I handled it. My supervisor thinks I am a good worker." Then the imaginary reward. The sequence was so clear that soon Jessy was creating her own imaginary scenes. And that was the point; that Jessy should control the whole process, from the determination of the stressor and the identification of the problem behavior, to the choice of the reward, taken from her treasury of Enthusiasms.

Like the contracts, the scenarios work by focusing attention. But with these too autism may shift the focus from the purpose of the process to the process itself. Jessy is delighted to talk about her scenes, which now (of course) have proliferated to several hundred. But she is as likely to fix on the multicolored paper clips that keep them neatly separate, or on the fact that a series has five cards rather than six, as on the problem behavior. Pattern, color, number — these are still the things that are intrinsically interesting, worth thinking about and talking about, over and over again.

Jessy has practiced her scenes daily since the early eighties, for like the contracts, they are no simple panacea. It is a lot easier to imagine a response than to summon it when needed, especially since in her intensest distress, Jessy doesn't *want* to relax. And although I'm not around when she goes through her cards — it's important that the process be self-administered — I can guess that a process so often repeated becomes a mechanical routine. Nevertheless, Jessy invokes it not less but more and more as she grows older. Caught up in some overreaction, to a what-question, to a cough or a sneeze, she'll say, "I must practice my scenes," and depart for her room to do just that. The cards empower her to control — not always, not entirely, but often — behavior that

Waiting for
People to get
Passed
(First Come First Serve)

I want to pass by or
use something, but someone
is there first.

I think to myself it's not 2
very long. I can do it.

I STOP & RELAX 3.

Reward!

Then let people finish 4
what they're doing.

I feel proud that I didn't 5
bonk people, knock on the
door, or barge in.

A sequence from Jessy's card system for relaxation.

would make it impossible for her to live and work in a normal community.

A few months ago I congratulated her on how much less she's been crying these days. "I can't remember," I told her, "the last time you cried." "October 14!" she says, then adds: "Must be the scenes *helped!*" And she's just created a new scenario, "Waiting for People to Get Passed (First Come First Serve)." "I want to pass by or use something, but someone is there first. I think to myself it's not very long. I can do it. I STOP and RELAX.

Reward! Then let people finish what they're doing. I feel proud that I didn't bonk people, knock on the door, or barge in."

Jessy's had a fine time while I've been writing this chapter. A delighted collaborator, she has happily listed for me her recent rewards. They are autism at its peculiar best. Jessy's rewards are nothing like the imaginary chocolate chip cookie June originally suggested. The twenty-nine items include, along with auroras and four kinds of eclipses, Route 7, south of Great Barrington and north of Manchester Center, and a "refrigerator set at vacation mode." The only one that is at all predictable is "double or more fortune Perugina Baci chocolates." We turn to the past: she may not have much interest in her old books, but she reads every word of the contracts — pluses, minuses, the record of almost two years of struggle. She regards it all with happy equanimity. I'm not surprised. I remember her comment on Darth Vader, who was famously bad but "turned out to be a good guy. I guess he learned from consequences! Like me!"

CHAPTER 11   "Guess what!
Some of the people at work
are my friends!"

Jessy is still learning from consequences. Now, however,
penalties and rewards arise naturally out of the situation — just
as they do for Darth Vader and the rest of us. If she's rude in the
restaurant, she won't get to go next week. But Jessy is no longer
limited to direct experience. Growth and the years continually
open up new avenues of social learning. There are movies; there's
TV. Above all there is print. The hard work of her teachers has
borne fruit. Jessy can read.

And she does read. Slowly willingness and skill increase
together, and with them knowledge and to some extent understanding of the world she lives in.

.   .   .

When school ended for Jessy some twenty years ago, her reading — after nine years of intensive effort — was just adequate for
simple, factual, predictable material. An unwelcome task at
school, at home it was limited to things with a clear payoff, like
cookie recipes. Without support, reading threatened to join the

174

other skills that had withered from lack of practice. Jessy had learned pottery, knitting, needlepoint, even weaving, from one young helper or another. All, though she had seemed to enjoy them, were abandoned when the companion left. She certainly didn't enjoy reading. Yet she needed to read daily, and not only recipes. She needed to read stories about people and the things they do. Yet the last story we'd read at home was a four-year-old's picture book, with no more than a few sentences of text.

But I remembered how she'd enjoyed reading the contracts. Those too were a kind of story, a story about Jessy and the things she did. That pointed the way. We would read as we had then, together, comfortable, warm and easy.

We read aloud, to rivet attention through both eye and ear. She resisted at first; I recognized the old inertia. But I didn't want to tackle it with a reward this time; that wasn't what reading was about. So I went back to earlier methods, luring her to read as I had lured the toddler who couldn't tolerate something missing into putting rings on a stick. Then I had put on all the rings but one; now I read, stopped, and Jessy supplied — she *had* to — the next word. First the next word. Then the next sentence. Then we took turns, so Jessy had to follow each sentence and couldn't tune out. *And then she began to follow the story within the sentences.* Touchingly, she asked for stories about "girls who misbehave."

We read book after book. Laura Ingalls Wilder's Little House series might have been designed to fill in the gaps for a person without a childhood. Not only does Laura misbehave, she grows, and the books with her. She's four in the first book, and her short, simple sentences were easy even for Jessy. Soon Jessy claimed as her own any paragraph that had Laura in it. She was less interested in personalities, of course, than the concrete things she could understand; to this day she can tell you about the long winter ("from November to the end of April") when the train couldn't get through and the Ingallses almost starved. But we pressed on through adolescence and got Laura married before we found Beverly Cleary's Ramona series. That was better yet; Ramona was five at the start and *really* misbehaved; she had tantrums and lay on her bed and kicked the wall. And as Ramona grew and went to school and struggled to control her temper so people would like her, Jessy's language and social comprehension expanded together. Year after year we went through series after series about girls and families, in the Midwest, in Norway, in Brooklyn, before we got to Dorothy and Oz. Then we stopped. Jessy didn't want me beside her anymore. She was probably tired of my running commentary — it was too much like a lesson. But she kept on reading.

Jessy has been reading Oz books ever since; so far she's read thirty. (There are thirty-seven in the series, and Jessy doesn't leave things unfinished.) She's read about witches, good and bad, about princesses and queens, about Polychrome the rainbow's daughter, who's particularly interesting to a colorist like Jessy. When she finishes a book she tells me the story, though as the plot dissolves in a jumble of details, my mind begins to wander. She enjoys the queens and witches, but what she *uses* is the information. When her interests turned from astrothings to real estate and banks, she was ready with what she'd learned from Oz. Banks lend money; Dorothy's Auntie Em and Uncle Henry lost their farm in Kansas when they couldn't pay the mortgage, and Auntie Em cried. Fortunate, then, that they could be transported to Oz, where, Jessy tells me, there isn't any money. Out of fantasy Jessy plucks realism; in Oz there are magic trees, but hanging on them are lunchboxes with ham sandwiches. In Oz she learns new words and concepts: "revenge" (tit for tat!), "enchantment," "oblivion."

Jessy has read about Willie Wonka and the chocolate factory, about James and the giant peach. But as with other autistic people, her primary interest is not in fiction but in fact. Oz is for vacations, when she has nothing else to do. But she scans every issue of *The Harvard Health Letter,* on the alert for items about drug side effects and the common cold. She checks out diseases in her medical encyclopedia. She reads the stories I've marked for her in the newspaper, her interests expanding from fees and ATM's and accidents on Route 7 to hurricanes in the tropics and blizzards in South Dakota. That's where the Ingallses had their problems, I remark, but Jessy supplies a nearer point of contact; her supervisor at work, an important person in her life, was stranded in South Dakota when the airport closed and has just got back. Maybe, Jessy suggests, we should send diapers and canned tuna fish to South Dakota; the news report says they are needed. So Jessy reads and thinks of others, as her world grows larger.

Like many for whom reading is hard and understanding partial, Jessy might be expected to prefer visual and auditory media. But it's even harder for her to extract meaning from movies and TV. The rapid images and talk defeat her slow information processing; what she hears are her "transition phrases." She understands the maps on the Weather Channel better than I do, but the spoken explanations are only words. As for movies, the ones she likes are based on books she knows already. Though she doesn't mine them for human relationships, insofar as they show her people in action they contribute their bit to Thinking of Others.

. . .

It would be natural to write here that as Jessy is more aware of others she is more aware of herself. Yet how she could be more aware of herself is hard for me to imagine. She drew a picture of

From left: Jessy (holding drawing of Piper Cleaner Man), Piper Cleaner Girl, Piper Cleaner Fairy, 1967.

herself before she could talk.[1] Among the Piper Cleaner people she placed herself as a major character. She even found a way to represent herself as their creator when she drew herself holding her drawing of Piper Cleaner Man. The picture with which she hailed her eleventh birthday is one of the treasures of the suitcase. JESSICA, she labeled it, in assertive capitals. It shows Jessy — *Jessica* — at eight, at nine, at ten, at eleven: four Jessies, four years of progress. For each Jessy is taller than the last.

As time went on and self-awareness could move from pictures to speech, she noted other kinds of growth. "I can't believe it, I read without being coaxed!" "I'm getting better at not insulting people" (her truthfulness compelled her to add, "Only did that last week"). "I had a speech handicap a long time ago." Who would correct such a comfortable assessment? Jessy's self-awareness usually is weighted toward the positive. She knows how sharp her hearing is, and often refers to it; she knows she has a remarkable sense of color. She is not at all surprised to find

Jessy at different ages, drawn to mark her eleventh birthday, 1969.

a story about herself in the paper. "Daddy found another announcement of my show!" Her smile is not an autistic, why-are-you-smiling smile; it is the smile of justified self-satisfaction.

Jessy is aware of her abilities and her progress. More surprising, in view of her incomprehension of other people's thoughts and feelings, is her awareness of her own mind. Mind, of course, is a highly abstract concept, and Jessy was sixteen when she first used the word. But she used it with an understanding that suggested the idea was not new to her. Looking at an old drawing of a tunnel in which her superball went "back and forth, back and forth," she told me where it happened — not in a real tunnel, but "in my mind." From then on it was a phrase she used freely; it allowed her to verbalize the difference she'd always recognized between the reality outside and the imaginary within.

Her self-awareness, of course, is intensified as I enlist her memories for this book. But even I am astonished by her consciousness of her mental history. Though I've asked her many questions, I never asked her where her wee-alo's came from; it didn't occur to me that she knew. So a few months ago I heard their origin for the first time: "I got that wee-alo's from the hellos at the end of the sentence" — the hellos that were extinguished a quarter-century ago. If she's aware of that, what else may she know?

She's aware of her dreams, too; if asked she will write them down. Often she illustrates them, and indeed they recall her earlier comic books. The plots, insofar as they exist, are sequential; there are no "dreamlike" discontinuities. They have generally upbeat endings. They are matter-of-fact even in fantasy. And they display plenty of "I."

> *First I went downstairs with the elevator to see some beautiful things. Then I went up to 8th floor. I waited for another elevator for 10th floor. It came and I went high into space. I said, "Come back elevator. I am lost in atmosphere." I saw the top of this building and came [back] to the 10th floor.*

Another, somewhat simpler:

> *I watched many cartoon movies about the swing set made of trees. Bears and other animals climbed onto it.*

Another:

> *I'm sick and tired of living on Hoxsey Street. I'm moving to Washington. I'm going to live in a friend's house.*

Like her comic books, her dreams are derivative rather than imaginative. Jessy drew the "swing set"; hung between trees, it

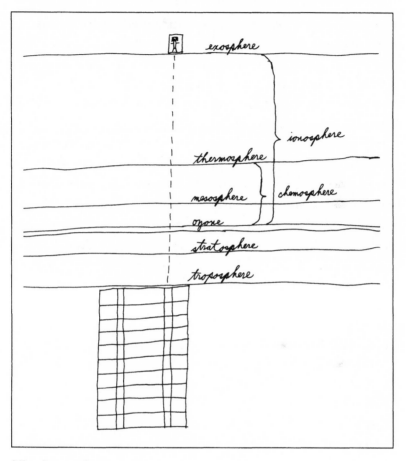

The elevator dream.

was recognizably the swing of her childhood. The animals are out of television. The vocabulary of her trip in space — her drawing of the dream had labels like "troposphere," "stratosphere," "mesosphere" — came from a scientific picture book. A friend once talked of a summer in Washington. Only the most hardened Freudian could convert such externalities into symbols.

There is something uncanny about a dream life so unmysterious, so close to the life of waking. But it is certainly self-aware.

. . .

Jessy is aware of herself, but there is a gap in her awareness. She is far more conscious of herself cognitively than emotionally. Mind — the word and the concept — came long before heart, though once she learned that hearts were something more than valentines or anatomical features they became a favorite topic. "I can't believe it, there are many ways to say '-hearted'! There's 'lighthearted,' 'heavyhearted,' 'downhearted,' 'brokenhearted,' 'chickenhearted,' 'lionhearted,' 'stouthearted,' 'good-hearted'!" It is possible to talk about emotions autistically; what these terms might actually mean is lost in the pleasing formalism. Encouraged to talk about "emotional feelings," Jessy readily adopts the new word, only recently distinguished from "motion" and still tinged with its meaning. Motion, moving. "I always walk fast if I'm happy and slow if I'm sad. Because of emotional feelings." She finds this worth thinking about, for next day, all smiles, she has more to add. "This is another reason about the emotional feelings. If my heart is light I can walk fast, if my heart is heavy I can walk slow. Because my feet will be heavy if I feel sad." Yet affairs of the heart, if you don't understand them, aren't really very interesting. Complacently, but only briefly, Jessy considers herself as an emotional being: "Boy, I never fell in love, with male or female!"

. . .

Jessy is not more self-aware as she begins to see herself in relation to others, but she is aware of herself differently. The self-involvement of autism diminishes, with obvious advantages. But with that comes — or *might* come — a source of pain. Does Jessy know she's different? It's a natural question; many people ask it. The answer is more complex than a simple yes or no, or even the "not yet" I put down when I first wrote about it almost twenty years ago.[2] It trails with it another, less natural question: not does she know, but does she care? What does autism — what does a mental handicap — mean to her?

Jessy was twenty-seven when an auto accident got us talking about the benefits of seat belts. I mentioned a child I knew of who had suffered brain damage in an accident before seat belts became mandatory. Jessy, showing some of her medical knowledge, at once picked up on the words "brain damage"; it could, she said, make you paralyzed. I said it could also make you retarded (as had indeed happened), so that you couldn't think very well or have a job. I could not have predicted Jessy's reaction. It was better to die in the accident, she said, than be — paralyzed, I expected, but instead she said "retarded." "Because then I couldn't have a good life." Clearly she had some idea of what it meant to be retarded — I suppose she'd heard the word at school. But just as clearly, her nine years in the special class had never suggested to her that it might be applied to herself.

To Jessy, handicaps are physical. A mental handicap is a perfect example of the kind of social generalization her mind has difficulty forming. She knows she took a long time to learn to talk and that she has to work hard to control her behavior — harder than other people. That's the way we've presented her difference to her. But the comparison is ours, not hers. To feel your own difference you have to form a concept of what other people are like, how they live, what's expected of them.

. . .

We had never tried to suppress the word "autistic," either in conversation or as it appeared in various publications about the house. Jessy had never asked about it. She knew there was a book about her; she had even typed the Spanish translation. There were no books about her siblings. She didn't wonder why; social comparisons were not within her scope. If she was to know she was autistic, we would have to tell her. The years went by and we didn't. She knew her problems; she went over them every day with her imagery scenes. It didn't seem necessary to give them a name.

Then, in 1988, *Rain Man* came along. That extraordinary movie made people in America and all over the world aware of a handicap few had known existed. We saw it and marveled at its accuracy and sensitivity. To prepare for his role Dustin Hoffman had spent weeks with two autistic young men — one was Joe Sullivan, whose multiplications and primes were so like Jessy's. Hoffman had absorbed the mumbles, the gait, the postures, the characteristic preoccupations of autism. He had sought expert advice; the film's credits were an honor roll of autism. Here was our opportunity. Jessy was thirty. Should we take her to see it?

We did. She saw it twice. It was the first adult movie — and so far the last — that she really enjoyed and understood. She recognized Rain Man's obsessions. "He was inflexible about his underwear," she told her brother. "And he stared at the dryer, clothes going round and round." He said "I don't know" a lot. He liked *Wheel of Fortune*. He mumbled. She could relate to it all, even feel a bit superior. "And he also farted in the telephone booth, and his brother said a bad word, a horrendous verbalization." *She* wouldn't do that — though her brother probably would. Jessy has known she is autistic ever since.

Many autistic adults greet their diagnosis with relief. It explains their problems; it may even put them in touch with others like

themselves. But they are less severely affected than Jessy; they feel
and understand things she does not. For Jessy autism is not a difficult social condition but a collection of specifics — mumbling,
crying, staring at things that go round and round. But those
specifics have led her forward; out of her awareness of autism
have come her first social generalizations.

"Well, I haven't cried for a whole month," she remarks. "Just
like the other adults." Then she adds, "I know some of the other
autistic people cried." Like other adults, like other autistic people.
Two comparisons — herself as normal (a word she has never
used), herself as autistic. Taking it further: "If I cry I always make
faces. If when people cry do they always make faces?" She's
thinking it through; she knows they don't. Later she will even
say, after one of her now rare mumbles, "Mother, I can't help it
because I'm one of the autisms." The generalization achieved,
Jessy has placed herself within it. But the odd diction gives her
away. Autism is a plural.

It is also a fact. Jessy takes it behavior by behavior, which is
probably the best way. Certainly it saves her a great deal of pain.
She doesn't suffer because she has no boyfriend. She doesn't yearn
for a baby. She has never asked why she is autistic, why, in the
searing words of one child, "God made me be like this." Jessy
knows who she is, and though she may wish she'd behaved differently in one case or another, she shows no sign of wanting to be
anything but what she is.

.   .   .

And yet, in the light of her awareness of her "autisms," she now is
able to say that she's ashamed. What are we to make of that?

Some cynic defined conscience as the little voice inside us
that tells us that someone is looking. His joke was deliberately to

confound inside with outside, conscience with shame. Our civilization tends to prefer conscience, to respect actions that arise from interior conviction above actions performed — or avoided — because of "what people will think." The parents of an autistic person, however, have a harder time admiring indifference to other people's opinions. Our child may not notice the stares and comments, but we do. And though we may be angry and inveigh against society's insensitivity, we begin to see the advantages of shame, and agree with Homer, who long ago said that it "does much harm to people but profits them also." For a person who doesn't care about what people think of her, one of the most effective human motivators is absent. If Jessy can say she is ashamed, if she experiences that bad feeling so familiar to most of us, if it hurts, if it makes her unhappy, surely it's to be welcomed as a huge step forward, an entrance into a new awareness of herself in society. If she can add actual real-world embarrassment to her STOP and RELAX and imagined rewards, mustn't their power be doubled?

Jessy says she's ashamed after she's done something egregious, like angrily snapping at an innocent what-question. It happens, though she's rehearsed her what-scenes more times than I could count. "What are you doing?" someone asked her not so long ago. He was a cameraman, and he needed to know. The words came at him like bullets: "Why do you ask me that?!" Then she whimpered, then she cried a bit, then she said, "I'm ashamed." So he caught on film what must, if we take it at face value, demonstrate exactly that concern for how she appears to others I've insisted is missing.[3] But those who know Jessy learn that the words she uses, even when they appear to suit the circumstances, do not always mean what they mean for us. The episode needs some digging; there is more to the story.

The innocent cameraman (of course he felt terrible about it) was part of a documentary team. They had been following us around for five days, guided by Dr. Oliver Sacks, and everything had gone more than well. They were shooting a six-part series on Dr. Sacks; Jessy was the center of attention of the autism section. She was filmed with her paintings, with an ATM machine, with the old sheets of flavor tubes. She was taken for a ride on her favorite routes. She loved it all. But then she snapped.

They got it on camera, and Jessy knew it. She knew that people would see it. And clearly, unambiguously, she said she didn't want it in the film. It wasn't the first time she'd said she was ashamed. But she'd never before said anything like that.

Of course they told her that if she didn't want it they wouldn't put it in. Months later, however, as the director, Christopher Rawlence, was putting together the footage, he realized that he needed Jessy's snap. To present autism as all charm and interesting strangeness was to romanticize it past recognition. We read Chris's letter to Jessy: though of course he would keep his promise to her, would she perhaps be willing to let him show her snapping, and crying, and being sorry? She said yes without a qualm — it was past, it was over, whatever she'd felt, whether embarrassment, shame, or simply the bad feeling that comes with disapproval. The snap went into the picture; it has been seen on both sides of the Atlantic. Chris sent us a video, and Jessy has watched it many times. She likes the route signs and the ATM. But the snap is her favorite part. She doesn't wince; she doesn't turn away. "I didn't know it was so *loud!*" she says — smiling.

I would like to think that the story of that snap contains some glint of a more fully social, more conscious future. But it pulls both ways; I don't know. This book will be long finished before I find out.

. . .

I do know, however, that the vocabulary of handicap doesn't work for Jessy. She doesn't "suffer from" autism. She doesn't think of herself as handicapped. "Afflicted" is a word she doesn't know. As in other things, she's matter-of-fact. She's well aware of her obsessions, whether she calls them enthusiasms or whether she calls them autisms and they get her into trouble. She's aware of her compulsions and rigidities and routines. She knows she must control them if she's to avoid . . . shame, perhaps, but certainly unpleasant consequences. She knows she needs consequences to do this, and imagery scenes, and what we call, and she calls, Flexibility Practice. She knows how important flexibility is to her daily life, and to what is perhaps its most important social element, her job.

Jessy was in her midteens before she could understand a concept like flexibility. But when she did, the phrase became another means to focus her mind on the importance of learning to accept the changes that upset her so. We'd been nudging her toward flexibility all through childhood: now we could talk about it. Altered schedules, unexpected guests, lost objects, overlong phone calls, power outages — no household can eliminate them, and no household should try. It's all too tempting, in the interests of peace and quiet, to imprison a whole family within the unbreakable routines that structure the lives of people with autism. To survive, families, and teachers — and employers — develop ways, not to avoid such disruptions, but to minimize the overreactions they trigger. Jessy can accept changes if she's told ahead of time; predicted, they can be absorbed into the reassuring order. (She can even accept a what-question if she knows it's coming.) "I will prepare myself." Negotiate the change in advance, allow her the time she needs to shift gears, and she can be flexible. Routines can be varied. In familiar areas, negotiation is no longer necessary, or rather, Jessy negotiates the adjustment with herself. It's another reason to feel proud of herself. "I was *flexible!*"

Inflexibility, of course, continues. Not every change can be predicted. Jessy gets used to working late at the busy startup of college, but when things calm down and overtime is only occasional she has to get used to it all over again. Best to recognize the uses of inflexibility, limited but real. Our household runs as smoothly as Jessy can make it. Though a quarter of a century has passed since she earned points for taking out the garbage, she has never once had to be reminded. Vitamin pills, accurately distinguished and distributed, appear by our plates every morning. At the risk of being nosy, Jessy checks the calendar for our appointments; she'll be more upset than we are if we forget one. We enjoy as fully as we can the accuracy and reliability that are the marks of her condition. They are valuable qualities, in the workplace as at home. Accuracy and reliability are what she brings to her job, the job that has been, and remains, Jessy's greatest social challenge.

.   .   .

It is also a challenge for everyone around her. Jessy's supervisor knows her as well as anyone outside her family and longtime companions. Though she has not studied autism, she is an expert. The employee evaluation forms she fills out could stand as a textbook review of autism's diagnostic indicators. "Jessy performs her work swiftly and thoroughly, if routines are not changed. She is a creature of habit, and does not like to be interrupted." So knowledge of the job, productivity, accuracy, and neatness are all marked Above Standard, as are punctuality and adherence to work schedules. There, however, the good news ends. "Jessy is unable to work without supervision." Initiative, ability to accept new procedures, acceptance of constructive suggestions, and adaptation to changing conditions are all marked Unsatisfactory. "Jessy follows daily routines, and dislikes changes in work conditions. She does not accept criticism well, and usually answers 'I don't know' [like Rain Man!] to most inquiries. She is unable to judge what to do in emergency situations."

Relationships with the public and other mailroom workers are Fair to Poor. "Jessy is friendly, but has the tendency to correct her student coworkers. We would hope that Jessy, in the future, could concentrate on her own work and leave corrections and supervisory matters to the designated individuals. She needs to be more polite with the students who use the mailroom." Jessy's supervisor is kind and patient. But there's a limit to the amount of patience we can or should expect. So we work hard with Jessy. Don't be nosy. Don't check the work on someone else's desk. Don't *touch* anything on someone else's desk, especially your supervisor's. Don't correct your coworkers; "be silent like a cat." *Be flexible*. And Jessy does her best; she tries hard to control her overreactions when somebody makes an error that anybody but Jessy would recognize as trivial. But though she can talk about getting her priorities right, it's hard for her to do it. She's known for twenty years that she *cannot* scream on the job; that she would certainly be sent right home and lose a day's pay; worse, that she might, in her own words, "get a pink slip." Though after twenty years that's probably not strictly true, it helps her to think so. Points long gone, the principle remains: there are some things that if they are to be controlled require a really significant penalty. As far as I know, this one has been effective; she has never screamed at work. Nor does she snap as she does at home. A workplace snap, in fact, provided one of her few "Knightmares."

"GUESS WHAT! SOME OF THE PEOPLE ARE MY FRIENDS!"

"I dreamt about snapping at work about what-questions, that I lost my job." I'm sorry about the nightmare, but I'm glad she cares about the possibility of a pink slip, that she knows how much she needs her job.

Jessy works a six-day week in the mailroom, 9 to 4:30 with a half day on Saturdays. Jessy's job provides the structure for her day, and for a life that, lacking ambitions and goals, is made up of days. It is her job, and only her job, that ensures daily contact with people outside her family. Her job, not her painting, is her greatest achievement. Her painting, however brilliant, is solitary. The job is social. I know of autistic adults with higher degrees who have been unable to get, or keep, the job for which their education seems to qualify them, because they have not adapted even as well as Jessy to the social requirements of the workplace. They are some of the unhappiest people I have ever seen.

.   .   .

There was a time when Jessy kept her journal regularly. In it she recorded, along with Discouragements, her Enthusiasms, even Ecstasies. I copy here two very different Ecstasies, because they are both work related, and because they express, better than I could, the satisfactions and challenges of autism. The first, dated 5/10/94, reads as follows:

> *The solar eclipse started at noon and ended at 3:30 PM. I looked through the Eclipse Shades, alternate with the pinhole cardboard. It was almost annular at 1:40. I noticed the shadows were sharper. The leaves were crescent.*

That, though it took place in working hours, was a wholly solitary ecstasy. Out on the grass outside the mailroom, surrounded

191

by people also looking heavenward, Jessy was alone, caught up in autism at its happiest, as the brightest and best of astrothings went into the rare wedding ring eclipse that would later find its way into a splendid painting. But autistic happiness is no better adapted to the workplace than autistic distress. Jessy, as I learned from her supervisor, was continually running in and out to check on the shadow's progress. Ecstasy meant the employee whose best attribute was reliability was not on the job.

A few months later, however, Jessy recorded another work-related Ecstasy. This one was at the opposite pole, not solitary, not a distraction from work, but social. "Just before going to bed," she wrote, "I got a 100% dinner invitation," the college's reward for employees who in a whole year had not missed a day of work. That Jessy was pleased, proud, that she went to the dinner and enjoyed it, that she was recognized as a good worker in a way she could understand — all that is a measure of social growth that could only take place in the context of her job. This year — incredible anniversary — she'll go to the luncheon for twenty-year employees. She'll go alone. Though I accompanied her to the 100 percent dinner, that was six years ago. I don't need to anymore. She knows how to do it now. There won't be much casual conversation, but she'll manage.

Still, social growth in autism is an uneven process. There's the student who told me that when Jessy smiles at him it makes his day. But there are also less encouraging incidents. Jessy went to the restroom one day, a year or so after the recognition dinner, and came back to find the chair she'd vacated occupied by a coworker. Without a word, she plumped herself down in the young woman's lap. It didn't make *her* day. "She criticized me," Jessy told me. I can imagine she did. Some things are funnier to read about than experience. But it is her supervisor, who observes so carefully and records so truthfully, who should have the last word on autism and employment. When she saw *Rain Man* she commented, "I don't see why he had to be in an institution. If Jessy can hold a job, he certainly ought to be able to." And with a lot of help, Jessy can.

. . .

Friendliness is learned among friends and social behavior in society. That society has opened up a place for Jessy is what, more than anything else, has made it possible for her to live in, even contribute to, the community she was born in. Ordinary people will be extraordinarily helpful when they know how much they contribute to Jessy's development. Storekeepers, bank tellers, checkout clerks, like supervisors and coworkers, will be patient, smile, and make allowances, as long as the behavior they see is not too disruptive and bewildering. They will smile out of the goodness of their hearts, and once they involve themselves they will smile because they see progress and know they have a part in it — a part more important than they can ever know. Let Jessy herself close the chapter:

"Guess what! Some of the people at work are my friends! Jim, and Betty, and Mary, and Diane, that pretty girl, and Ginny, and Karl, and Carol that I pounded on the door, and Gary who is fat but I won't say that to him. And I will make them all paperweights for Christmas!"

CHAPTER 12   Valedictory

"I will make them paperweights." It comes out easily, as it should. It feels easy, in her mouth and at her painting table, where soon she will transform beach stones into colorful gifts. Jessy's used to giving Christmas presents. But of course the giving of presents, like any other social transaction, is easy only if you know how. Even for normal people, Thinking of Others requires education. Jessy's learned the general principle: you should do it. But that's quite different from applying it in particular cases.

Seven years ago, entirely spontaneously, Jessy gave me a Mother's Day present. I was accustomed to Mother's Day cards; Jessy never misses a holiday. But I wasn't expecting a present. I certainly wasn't expecting this one. Elegantly wrapped, it contained a can of cat litter deodorizer — Jessy takes care of the litter pan — and one of those little give-away packets of strawberry jam.

Now, Jessy's not a tightwad. She long ago became acclimated to taking money out of the bank as well as putting it in. She was perfectly willing to contribute five thousand dollars to the renovation of our kitchen. But with the best will in the world, Thinking of Others runs into problems if you haven't got a working theory of mind. So most of the time we prompt and suggest. Painted paperweights, one step up from cards. For very special friends, a painting. Repeated suggestions become internalized; for birthdays, Jessy knows we all like a homemade cake (although if it's to be anything but chocolate we put in a special order). Beyond that, it's best to follow the example of Anna and Diana, always practical, who specify exactly what to buy and where.

. . .

The experience of autism has many ports of entry. Presents are as good a way as any to begin this valedictory chapter, the chapter of Where Is Jessy Now? Categories bleed; Strange morphs into Ordinary, and back into Strange again. Or we can reverse the terms, since with Jessy they have no clear boundaries. If it ends with Ordinary, it will still be Strange enough.

. . .

The identification of suitable presents is a regular pre-Christmas activity for Jessy, and for us as well. If practice doesn't make perfect, still, as we talk about friends and the things they like, individualities come into sharper focus. Rachel likes cats; Drew likes football; Betty likes flowers. Different people like different things. But finding the right present for Jessy herself presents its own challenges. Rachel likes cats, but what does *she* crave? Back in Nirvana the two-year-old wanted nothing enough even to reach for it. Even now, any one of us could list ten desires for every one of Jessy's. Forget jewelry. Forget clothes; her attitude toward them is strictly utilitarian. Records, once "too good" to listen to, she now doesn't play at all. Stars and rainbows, the old standbys, are too familiar to cause a thrill. But study her current enthusiasms. How about a birthday cake iced as a bank? A copy of *The Physicians' Desk Reference for Nonprescription Drugs*? A medical dictionary? Find the right present, and Jessy's face will light up to illuminate us all.

Her siblings, with forty years of experience, are artists in choice. Sheets emblazoned with Hershey's Kisses. Sweatshirts bearing her own magic phrases. An assortment of cold remedies. And, this Christmas, a stroke of genius: a regime, a *system* of skin care. An array of tiny bottles, face creams, body creams, lotions; a brochure of complicated instructions for each; night/day, dry/oily, sensitive/normal; permutations and combinations, endless material for contemplation — and conversation, for Jessy's enthusiasms are no longer too good to utter. All unbelievably expensive — except that the little bottles were advertising samples and the brochure was free.

The cosmetics company, however, lost nothing by such generosity. Jessy's next stop after Christmas is urgent; the person who craved nothing (unless you count chocolate) has something to buy. Where is she now? She is at the mall at opening time, engaged in what is surely a typical, age-appropriate American activity, shopping. There are no other customers so early, which is fortunate, because Jessy requires the sales clerk's undivided attention. Society, in its representative, reaches out with kindly interest to this forty-year-old woman who speaks so laboriously yet asks such well-informed questions. Can you use the day cream for night? What will happen if you switch the creams for dry and normal? She's spent hours over that brochure; she's mastered every detail. She's searching for a rational system, which the charts suggest exists, but which of course doesn't. Encouraged by me, the salesperson concedes you can switch creams, it doesn't really matter. But Jessy insists; rules are what a regime is all about. The minutes tick past.

Jessy wants a particular bottle; the saleswoman looks everywhere and finally finds it in a drawer. After an hour I can't stand it anymore; gently I bring the transaction to a close, pointing out that other customers are beginning to arrive. Jessy has spent a happy hour and seventy-six dollars; later, in another store, she'll spend fifty dollars more to fill out the set. And no, she still doesn't look in the mirror. Why should she?

. . .

I write, and anecdotes are all around me, new ones every day. Few of them, by now, are even as bizarre as this one. Everything she does is what she is; everything she does encapsulates the absorption of autism into the everyday. As I press to conclude a story that can have no real conclusion, I find a slip from the very week I began this book — one more record, a minuscule triumph. It's breakfast time. Jessy has filled the kettle, brought it to a boil, and taken it upstairs to flush out the bathtub drain, a self-appointed weekly routine. I've sat down to read the paper, since the kettle isn't there for me to make tea as I usually do. And now she's back with the empty kettle; I ask her can she make my tea, and get her cheerful, confident "Sure." She's done parts of the process before, so I know the job isn't beyond her. Still, I'm impressed. I'm not even looking at her, I'm absorbed in the paper, and she's refilled the kettle, set it to boil, gotten the teapot, put in the right amount of tea, set the pot above the kettle to warm, poured in the boiling water, and left it to steep. She's gone when I look up — it's time to leave for work, and Jessy's always on time. But to crown it all, when I come to pour the tea — *real* tea, not a wilted tea bag — there beside my cup is the tea strainer. I never asked for that, it's not part of the process. But I always use it. *She noticed!*

Such a commonplace incident. *That's the point.* Categories bleed. Strange into Commonplace, Talking, Thinking, Painting, Living, blended and inseparable. The same week I find she's put away the onions and potatoes "without told." I articulate it for her: "You don't have to wait for me to tell you, you can do it for yourself." More and more she can, and does.

A week later: I congratulate her not for a new accomplishment but for something she *hasn't* done. It's been two days, and she hasn't mentioned my cold. Of course I've hidden it as best I can, but she's noticed it; I know because she took away my cloth napkin and substituted a paper one. *And she hasn't said anything.* But now she beams; she reports she's been practicing the cold scene slowly — S-T-O-P, R-E-L-A-X — so she didn't have to cry. Or even snap. At last, she's really using the scenes as they are meant to be used, for self-management, for easier, happier, ordinary living.

She won't be, can't be, fully independent, but she's more independent every year. Two years ago she was anxious at the very mention that her father and I might take a trip: "But who will stay with me?" But last year she stayed alone for two nights, having found it much more convenient to sleep in her own bed than at her brother's. This year, when the housemates who hold the fort when we are on vacation asked was it okay for them to move into the dorms when school started, she answered, "Sure!" Compulsions too are absorbed into daily life, may even become tinged with Thinking of Others. As I finish one bottle of vitamin drops, she opens the new one, knowing I have trouble with the child-proof cap — having previously made sure, a week ahead, to buy the replacement, as the mental energy that once poured into the creation of systems flows constructively into forward planning. She's decided, she tells me, to omit the canonical bacon from her

Sunday breakfast; she'll need it to make the chowder tomorrow. Her heavy investment in order organizes the future, and we reap the benefits. She's even being flexible.

The book progresses; it's almost done when proudly she shows me a new scene. She's titled it Thinking of Others and secured the cards with a lime-green paper clip. "I will think of others beside myself," she writes carefully, and then, astonishingly, "I will think of how people feel." She can't make it more specific than that, and the applications will remain problematic. But the thought does count, and she deserves her imagined reward.

And yet — there's always a yet — compulsions remain compulsions, perhaps all the more noticeable in their everyday setting. Jessy arrives back from work tense in every muscle; there was so much mail she forgot to drink water at 11:30. She'd given blood the day before, and the nurse told her to double her fluid intake for forty-eight hours. I help her say the words: "No big deal." But it *is* a big deal for her; she echoes another soothing phrase, "People *do* forget," but her angry voice belies the verbal acceptance. Still tense, she decides "I will skip it" — that being what her drug manual recommends for a missed pill. It takes a good deal of logic to persuade her that if she wants to double her fluid intake skipping's not the way. Autism is a lifetime condition.

. . .

These days, however, most of her discouragements and satisfactions are like those of other people — less interesting to read about than the joys and anxieties of her private universe, yet reassuring in their very ordinariness. Life for all of us is full of commonplace annoyances — things break, the hot water runs out when we're in the shower. Jessy overreacts to these, and if she thinks she's alone she may still invoke one of her bizarre phrases: "Oh well about the water hang hang!" But life is also full of ordinary pleasures — chocolate chip pancakes, shared laughter, the return of friends. Such pleasures are less intense than the pleasures of Nirvana. But Jessy doesn't spend much time in Nirvana anymore. Though Ecstasies are enveloping while they last, they don't last long. She'll happily emerge to tell us about them — if we don't ask why she is smiling.

Thus life blends strange and ordinary, however the proportions change. Job, daily tasks, cookies to bake, perhaps even dinner to cook — Jessy is busy. And painting. How ordinary is that? She paints buildings now, and buildings are certainly more ordinarily found in paintings than the heaters and radio dials and electric blanket controls that were her chosen subjects fifteen years ago. And yet her buildings are extra-ordinary. The incandescence of their colors escapes the finest reproduction. There's a rainbow in the boarding of a barn, set off, below the drainpipe that appears in so many of her paintings, against a deep, pure red. A small, high window is — let her tell it — "purplish ultramarine." The sky behind a multicolored skyscraper is strange too: "two different shades of salmon," because "cloud disrupt the blending of stratification."

Such colors seem so surreal that we like to imagine we are seeing the colors of her secret world. And in a sense we are; rainbows were for years a major Enthusiasm, and even now there are few paintings that don't include some version of the full spectrum. Nevertheless, Jessy insists on the plainness of fact; she tells those who ask that she sees the same colors they do, just changes them to "make it more beautiful." Similarly, if the inclusion of a drainpipe seems strange, it is our eye, not Jessy's, that has turned autistic literalism into surreality. The drainpipe is not emotion-charged but ordinary; it is there because it was *there,* as her foot was there as she looked at her father in his wicker chair. Nor does it occur to her that there is anything odd about the migraine lightning behind her church. Lightning is lightning and migraine is migraine; why not combine the two?

If the paintings open into her private universe — and they do — it is only secondarily through the color that reaches us. What reaches her, what illuminates the painstaking hours spent with her tubes and brushes, is the obsessional material. Shades of salmon are good, but what sets her smiling is the stratification. The word, with its many syllables, is a recent acquisition, but the Enthusiasm is not. *Layers* have been special ever since the days when she thrilled to road construction and pebblestones and tar. Heaters were special; lampposts were special; odometers were special; there are paintings of them all. Merrill Lynch and Godiva are special still, doubly special if you put them together. Left to herself, Jessy would paint an ATM machine; one day she probably will. It's such happy obsessions ("*all* obsessions are good") that make visible the emotional intensity of her secret life. Realizing that, we realize that as we no longer even dream of a triumphant emergence into normality, we no longer even want her to exit Nirvana all the way. In a development we could never have envisaged, it looks as if she, and we, can have it both ways. Through art she can keep in touch with the underground springs of her emotional life without threatening her life in the everyday — that emotional life that is so much more thrilling than our own. It's a life she has no words for, but it's part of — perhaps it's at the bottom of — her oddly resistant happiness. Even if we could, we wouldn't deny her that.

Yet painting, with its bills and checks and record keeping, is very much part of the everyday. Jessy paints, paintings bring checks, the numbers rise in her bank account as they once rose on her golf counter. The checks are a significant motivator for her, as the growing recognition is for us, who must answer inquiries and learn to negotiate the world of galleries and shows — social complexities forever beyond Jessy's ken. But for us, and for her, what's important about this demanding, absorbing activity, valued and rewarded by society, is not what it brings to her bank account or her reputation (a concept much harder to understand than stratification), but what it brings to her life. It interests people, predisposes them in her favor, encourages them to overlook behavior that needs overlooking. In autism, that's important. Yet her painting's real meaning for her life is even more ordinary. It gives her something to do. Something to do when she's not forwarding mail, or changing the cat's pan, or mending her clothes, or changing her sheets, or attending aerobics (a scheduled, repetitive, predictable, satisfying autistic activity), or making applesauce, or, as they say, whatever. But there isn't any whatever for Jessy. Her expanded skills do not and cannot embrace the huge range of normality; she doesn't know what to do with leisure. With nothing to do, she won't go for a walk or call a friend. She reverts to the old, stereotyped behaviors. She still likes to rock.

So it is that her real achievements are in the realm of the practical, the necessary, the unromanticizable — the things that make her employable in the community and useful and welcome at home. How important it was that as a baby, however indifferent she was to others, she be attractive to them: clean, nicely dressed, no runny nose, no disgusting habits. We worked hard on that. Today she is still attractive, though not as lovely as that golden baby. Not that she cares. She has her hair cut unbecomingly short as soon as summer comes; when I suggest it's nicer long she says it's cooler. She dresses neatly, but it's not from any interest in her appearance that she lays her clothes out so carefully the night before; it's because if she feels hurried in the morning, if she sleeps a single minute past seven-fifteen, she will be intensely, irrationally distressed at the deviation from this one of the many routines that structure and maintain her world.

Routine, autism's curse and gift. Jessy is at ease only when what's to be done is done. The distresses of deviation are balanced by the reliability and exactitude that make her an efficient mail clerk, and the daughter I couldn't do without. Once there was no motivation, then there were points, now there is routine. Does she enjoy these tasks? The question is meaningless. She does them because she does them, because she is radically uncomfortable if they are left undone. However trying her compulsiveness may be for those around her, routine gets the work done, makes life livable.

Nor is routine incompatible with creativity; routine maintains the growing beauty of her paintings. Once a commission is received and a painting begun, it must be completed, perfectly, to the last barely visible detail. Is that all there is to it? Here too the years have been about growth, not just growth in technique, but growth in what for want of a better word I must call sociality. When her work was first exhibited, years ago in a little local gallery, she was interested only in the refreshments. She is still interested in the refreshments, but now she also enjoys the praise. When people come to the house, she says, "Do you want to see my paintings?" and makes sure they look at every one. In 1993 a tiny reproduction of one of them was chosen to represent Massachusetts on the White House Christmas tree. When we showed her the story in the paper, she exclaimed, "So it's the first time the president to hear from *me!*" Let this be the measure of her entry into the world we share.

The point, of course, is not to make her a willing drudge, at home, at work, or at her painting table. The point, now as always, is to maintain and expand the range of activity that makes her what we never thought she could be, a busy, useful member of the household and community. She'll be late in her forties, probably, her siblings into their fifties, when her future becomes their responsibility. Whether she stays in her own home with a companion or moves to a group home or a sheltered village or lives with a brother or sister, her active usefulness will make the road smoother both for her and for those around her.

It is not only because she is useful, however, that I can write these words with a faith in a future I will not see. Usefulness is a tremendous achievement — her own, and that of all who have accompanied her on the difficult road to activity and self-control. But it is not for her usefulness that people love her, with a love that is that future's best guarantee. They love her for her other-worldliness, her simplicity, her utter incapacity for manipulation or malice. They love her for her childlike purity.

Childlike. I have held off from using that word, although it must have occurred more than once to anyone reading my careful transcriptions of things that Jessy has said. For all the talk of "discovering the child within us," it is thought condescending, lacking in respect, to compare a mentally handicapped adult to a child. But those who have lived with Jessy know that the truest respect lies not in the wishful insistence that she is really just like other people, but in the recognition, and the valuing, of what she is.

· · ·

Arbeiten und lieben — to work and to love; were these not Freud's measures of success? Jessy has learned to work, even to prefer activity to idleness. A golf counter made this possible, and it seemed a miracle. But no clicking mechanism can teach love.

When I first wrote the Jessy story, thirty-four years ago, I made "love" the final word. Love, ours and other people's, is the condition of Jessy's life, little as she would be able to understand that. What, then, does love mean to her, and what does it mean if I write that she has learned to love? Twenty years ago, when her sister was long away and Jessy had shown no sign of noticing, she said out of nowhere, "I am missing her." She didn't say the word "love" then; like other emotion-words, it's not part of her effective vocabulary. But I can guess how she loves, or rather, I don't have to guess. She made it plain ten years later, in one of her "I hope you will feel better" responses to the unwelcome fact of illness. She said it, for some reason, not with annoyance but unusual sweetness. She even elaborated: "I can't give you a hug, because you have a cold." I told her that what she said was a verbal hug, that it made me happy because I love her and she loves me. She picked it right up, generalizing, exploring: "And my brother loves me, because he got up from my favorite seat." That was all, and I haven't heard her say the word again. But it was enough; love for her is its concrete manifestations. And she's not wrong. "He that would do good to another must do it in Minute Particulars," wrote William Blake.

. . .

The anecdote that must end this account is about love, and an event that told me more than I knew about where Jessy is today. Though Jessy is a happy person, it is not a happy story, but it is a good one. It comes in two parts.

Of all the young people who have loved Jessy and helped her grow, there is no one who helped her more, and loved her better, than Marilyn. Marilyn lives in Oakland now, working with the deaf; we like to think Jessy contributed to that. In 1991 there was a fire in Oakland. We pointed out the picture to Jessy when the

TV news came on, making sure she knew Mal was safe. The next day, when she asked, "Should I cry if I found out Mal is dead?" we were startled but not surprised. Jessy, who must try so hard to control her crying, often asks, "Is it a good reason to cry?"

A few seasons later, she was enjoying a new acronym — one of the repeatable, manageable formalisms that help her gain a hold on the uncertainties of the world. TBA: she knows that from the college calendar — To Be Arranged, so helpful when things may not occur as scheduled. She had been planning to go visit her friend Scooch, one of the dearest of the long succession of those who've lived with Jessy. Scooch didn't forget her when he graduated from Williams. As his own career carried him into the art world, he made her career his project. He commissioned a painting of his grandfather's house. He took her to sketch it, but it was raining and she couldn't. He was going to take her again. But he was busy and troubled, more troubled than we knew. The weeks wore on. Jessy doesn't like to wait, but she can handle it with TBA; TBA makes her smile.

Then comes the telephone call I can still hardly believe. Scooch is dead.

Shall we tell Jessy? We decide we must; she'll have to know sometime. She doesn't say anything, but goes to her room. I don't know why I don't follow her. I guess my own emotions are too raw. I can't bear to hear what she might say. The next day she tells me she "cried silently"; that's how she's supposed to cry at work, if she must cry, and certainly I didn't hear her. She asks some questions about what she's calling "the death." They are factual, neutral; they are at least endurable. She doesn't want to go with us to the funeral, and we don't press her.

We'll have a memorial gathering, it's decided, just his closest friends, here at the island he loved. We'll plant a flowering bush.

Jessy will be with us. They all know about her. So she won't get bored or impatient, I tell her what's going to happen; we'll dig the hole, plant the bush, and stand about it and remember Scooch. Anybody who wants to can say something.

I consider feeding her something appropriate to say, but decide against it. The rest of us speak what we feel, then are silent.

Minutes pass. *And then Jessy begins to speak.* I paraphrase; it was not a time for note-taking. Quietly, factually, she tells the things Scooch did for her, that he organized her first one-man show, that he got her a commission to paint the National Arts Club on Gramercy Park, that he took her to sketch the Flatiron Building and the beautiful church, that he took her to New Jersey to sketch his grandpa's beautiful house but she couldn't because it was raining and even the photographs weren't good, that they were going to go back but it was TBA. In her tone was neither the cheerfulness none of us could have borne, nor autistic desolation, but quiet sadness.

Happiness isn't everything. Jessy knows, I think, in her own concrete way, that her friend did those things for her because he loved her. He loved her innocence, her pure transparency; he saw it in her paintings. He loved the fact that words like "innocence" mean nothing to her; that transparency to her is only a property of glass. He loved her, he made her happy, she won't see him again. And that is a good reason to cry.

Afterword

Jessy cannot tell her story for herself. Though she can speak nothing but truth and her memory is unerring, I must tell it for her, today as when she was eight years old. She has learned to read, but she will never read it. Once I was naive enough to think she might; when I wrote that account of her first eight years I changed her name to Elly so she need never be embarrassed. I know now how effortful is her reading, how partial her understanding, how questionable her embarrassment. I know too that she'd never read such a story even if she could, or understand why it might be worth the telling. So I can tell it freely, in its continuing strangeness and its increasing, precious ordinariness, as Jessy enters, more and more fully, yet never entirely, the world in which we live, all of us, together.

APPENDIX I Jessy's Descriptions of
Some of Her Paintings

J essy began writing descriptions of her paintings in 1980, the year she finished school, as a way of maintaining and extending her hard-won writing skills. The first descriptions depended heavily on prompts and suggestions. Gradually she learned more and more about what a viewer might need to be told; still, it was some years before she wrote one independently. She has written her descriptions independently ever since. Though she writes a draft in pencil and asks me to look it over, only occasionally do I suggest an addition or revision in the interests of clarity. These examples are her descriptions of the paintings reproduced in color in this book.

"The Great Stained Glass Doors in Spring at Dawn" #10 (5/1/89)

These windows are in Aunt Adrienne's house in Brooklyn. The doors slide open and close. There's a shadow on right-hand panel. The doors open on three hinges. The floor that is the closest is made of wood. I made it brick red instead of brown just to make it interesting. The floor that is behind it is made of slate tile. The fence was a neutral color, but I made it lilac with light purple lines. The tree is in the yard. The sky is pink. The picture is in April 1989.

Jessy Park

209

St. Paul's and St. Andrew's Methodist Church and the Migraine Type Lightning and the Elves (10/17/98)

This is St. Paul's and St. Andrew's Methodist Church on 86th street and West End Avenue of Manhattan. The sky has five layers of blue. The glowing doughnuts all over the sky are elves. Elves are leftover from the night before. I painted the night before, in a painting of the Con Ed building. In that painting the sky had the jellyfish-shaped blob, sprites and jets. In this painting it is the morning after and there are only elves. You can read about sprites, jets, and elves in the article from Science News, December 23/30, 1995. The three very pale lavender, mint, and yellow zigzagging objects are lightning. They look white, but they are three different pastels. I made up this kind of lightning, because I see them when I have migraine. The third and fourth layers of the sky, counting up from the bottom, are wider than the night before, in the other painting. That night there was a band of cloud, but it disappeared in this painting.

This church is old. There are many broken pieces, dented metal, and broken window panes. If you look at the outer border of round windows, you can see the broken area in two places. There are also some broken pieces in the scallop section below the windows in the tower. There is a missing face above the center window. If you look further up, you can see five red faces. This is the second version of the church of St. Paul and St. Andrew. The first version has a cloudy sky and different colors.

Jessy Park

George Washington Bridge with the
Light Pillar Reflections (2/1/99)

    This is a painting of George Washington
Bridge, looking from the helicopter. If you look
at the sea, you can see the reflected light pillars.
On the bridge there are two buses, one truck, four
sport utility vehicles, and rest of them are cars.
Look for the gold car and the silver car. If you
look just below one of the light pillar reflections,
you can see the fake lighthouse. The magenta
objects inside the arch is the toll plaza. A yellow
car is at the toll booth. If you look on the back,
there is a copy of the light pillars.

Jessy Park

The Flatiron Building with the Rosy Light
and the Pinkish Lightning (9/26/99)

This is the Flatiron Building from the view of the 30th floor of the building across. I put a rainbow called the rosy light, instead of other buildings and streets. If you look through the windows, you can see the pinkish lightning. Also the window panes make the sky a little redder, if you look through. The lightning started off thick at the top window. Then it divided and thinned at the big window. There is one lightning at the bottom window of the picture. One of the top windows has the shade half way down, and one of them has the shade down a bit. Lower part of the big windows have the venetian blinds a part way down. On one of the three windows has the blind down open, and two have the blind down closed. The yellows on the bottom windows are slightly different from the upper windows. On the left of the big windows is the woman's face, and on the right is the man's face. Above right from the male face, you can see a little sculpture like thing.

Jessy Park

APPENDIX II Definitions

DSM IV Definition of Autism

These are the American Psychiatric Association's diagnostic criteria for Autistic Disorder, as laid out in the *Diagnostic and Statistical Manual of Mental Disorders,* fourth ed. (Washington, D.C.: American Psychiatric Association, 1994), pages 70–71 and 77–78.

A. A total of six (or more) items from (1), (2), and (3), with at least two from (1), and one each from (2) and (3):
1. qualitative impairment in social interaction, as manifested by at least two of the following:
    a. marked impairment in the use of multiple nonverbal behaviors such as eye-to-eye gaze, facial expression, body postures, and gestures to regulate social interaction
    b. failure to develop peer relationships appropriate to developmental level
    c. a lack of spontaneous seeking to share enjoyment, interests, or achievements with other people (e.g., by a lack of showing, bringing, or pointing out objects of interest)
    d. lack of social or emotional reciprocity
2. qualitative impairments in communication, as manifested by at least one of the following:
    a. delay in, or total lack of, the development of spoken language (not accompanied by an attempt to compensate through alternative modes of communication such as gesture or mime)
    b. in individuals with adequate speech, marked impairment in the ability to initiate or sustain a conversation with others
    c. stereotyped and repetitive use of language or idiosyncratic language
    d. lack of varied, spontaneous make-believe play or social imitative play appropriate to developmental level
3. restricted repetitive and stereotyped patterns of behavior, interests, and activities, as manifested by at least one of the following:

a. encompassing preoccupation with one or more stereotyped and restricted patterns of interest that is abnormal in intensity or focus
b. apparently inflexible adherence to specific, nonfunctional routines or rituals
c. stereotyped and repetitive motor mannerisms (e.g., hand or finger flapping or twisting, or complex whole-body movements)
d. persistent preoccupation with parts of objects

B. Delays or abnormal functioning in at least one of the following areas, with onset prior to age 3 years:
1. social interaction,
2. language as used in social communication, or
3. symbolic or imaginative play

C. The disturbance is not better accounted for by Rett's Disorder or Childhood Disintegrative Disorder

The association's definitions of Asperger's disorder and PDD-NOS (Pervasive Developmental Disorder Not Otherwise Specified) depend on the previous definition. The criteria for Asperger's disorder are almost identical, except for the *absence* of "clinically significant general delay" in "language . . . [or] in cognitive development or in the development of age-appropriate self-help skills, adaptive behavior (other than in social interaction), and curiosity about the environment in childhood." PDD-NOS may be diagnosed "when there is a severe and pervasive impairment of reciprocal social interaction or verbal and nonverbal communication, or when stereotyped behavior, interest, and activities are present" but the criteria for "atypical autism" or another specific disorder are not met. Autism may be called atypical "because of late onset, atypical symptomatology, or subthreshold symptomatology, or all of these."

The Autism Society of America Definition of Autism

This is the definition of autism that appears in every issue of the Autism Society's newsletter, *The Advocate*.

Autism is a complex developmental disorder that typically appears in the first three years of life. The result of a neurological disorder that affects the functioning of the brain, autism and its related disorders have been estimated to occur in as many as 1 in 500 individuals. Autism is four times more prevalent in boys than girls and knows no racial, ethnic, or social boundaries. Family income, lifestyle, and educational levels do not affect the chance of autism's occurrence.

Autism interferes with the normal development of the brain in the areas of social interaction and communication skills. Children and adults with autism typically have difficulties in verbal and nonverbal communication, social interactions, and leisure and play activities. The disorder makes it hard for them to communicate and relate to the outside world. They may exhibit repeated body movements (hand-flapping, rocking), unusual responses to people or attachments to objects, and they may resist changes in routines.

Over one half million people in the U.S. today have some form of autism. Its prevalence rate now places it as the *third* most common developmental disability — more common than Down syndrome.

Useful Publications

Books

There are now more books on autism than anyone can read. The best introduction to their range is the 200-title list available from the Autism Society of North Carolina Bookstore at 505 Oberlin Road, Suite 230, Raleigh, NC 27605–1345. Tel: (919) 743–0208. Web site: **www.autismsociety-nc.org**. It includes all the titles below and most of the others cited in the text.

Cohen, Shirley. *Targeting Autism: What We Know, Don't Know, and Can Do to Help Young Children with Autism and Related Disorders* (Berkeley: University of California Press, 1998). A realistic and readable survey of autism and its current treatments. Cohen describes an encouraging number of helpful educational programs, but remains skeptical of claims of cure.

Grandin, Temple. *Thinking in Pictures and Other Reports from My Life with Autism* (New York: Doubleday, 1995). A successful and articulate professional, Grandin gives significant insights into the abilities and disabilities of autism.

Frith, Uta, ed. *Autism and Asperger Syndrome* (Cambridge: Cambridge University Press, 1991). Six experts on autism describe autism and Asperger's syndrome and consider their overlap. Contains Asperger's original paper.

Hart, Charles. *Without Reason: A Family Copes with Two Generations of Autism* (New York: Harper & Row, 1989). How autism affected the author's uncle in the days before diagnosis and treatment, and how it has affected his son.

McDonnell, Jane Taylor. *News from the Border: A Mother's Memoir of Her Autistic Son* (New York: Ticknor & Fields, 1993). A vivid account of the development of an autistic child into an adolescent and young adult struggling to enter the normal world. Includes a valuable afterword by Paul McDonnell.

Maurice, Catherine. *Let Me Hear Your Voice: A Family's Triumph over Autism* (New York: Ballantine Books, 1994). A mother's detailed account of her two children's successful treatment by intensive behavioral methods. An informative and hopeful story that earns trust by its refusal to claim the method as a universal cure.

Pollak, Richard. *The Creation of Dr. B: A Biography of Bruno Bettelheim* (New York: Simon & Schuster, 1997). A fascinating examination of the career of the man whose influence did so much to retard the understanding and treatment of autism.

Powers, Michael D., ed. *Children with Autism: A Parents' Guide* (Kensington, Md.: Woodbine House, 1989). A comprehensive introduction. Extensive lists of national and state resources.

Schopler, Eric, ed. *Parent Survival Manual: A Guide to Crisis Resolution and Related Developmental Disorders* (New York: Plenum Press, 1995). Combining the experience of professionals and parents, this short, practical book is crammed with ingenious suggestions for dealing with the problems that arise in every aspect of daily life with an autistic child.

Seroussi, Karyn. *Unraveling the Mystery of Autism and Pervasive Developmental Disorder: A Mother's Story of Research and Recovery* (New York: Simon and Schuster, 2000). A far-reaching exploration of the possible role of diet in the treatment of autism.

Siegel, Bryna. *The World of the Autistic Child: Understanding and Treating Autistic Spectrum Disorders* (New York: Oxford University Press, 1996). Comprehensive and thorough, Siegel's book is richly packed with examples from her wide clinical experience.

Wing, Lorna. *Autistic Children: A Guide for Parents and Professionals* (New York: Brunner-Mazel, 1985). Dr. Wing explains autism with the authority of a professional and the understanding of a parent.

Periodicals

Autism Research Review International, Bernard Rimland, ed. Summarizes research in specialized journals; special interest in nutritional treatments. Published quarterly by Autism Research Institute, 4182 Adams Avenue, San Diego, CA 92116.

Journal of Autism and Developmental Disabilities, Gary B. Mesibov, ed. Scholarly reports of highly specialized research; reviews of current books. Published quarterly by Plenum Press, 233 Spring Street, NY 10013.

The MAAP: A Quarterly Newsletter for Families of More Advanced Individuals with Autism, Asperger Syndrome, and Pervasive Developmental Disorder,

Susan Moreno, ed. Perspectives on the problems and possibilities of high-functioning autism, written by parents, professionals, and autistic people themselves. Published by MAAP Services, Inc., P.O. Box 524, Crown Point, IN 46308. Web site: **www.maapservices.org**.

NAARRATIVE: Newsletter of the National Alliance for Autism Research. Updates on research, legislation, and other issues concerning autism. Published by National Alliance for Autism Research, 414 Wall Street, Research Park, Princeton, NJ 08540. Toll-free tel. (888) 777-NAAR. Web site: **www.naar.org**.

Published Materials About Jessy

Bogyo, Lola, and Ronald Ellis. "Elly: A Study in Contrasts," in *The Exceptional Brain,* L. K. Obler and D. Fein, eds. (New York: Guilford Press, 1988).

Park, Clara Claiborne. "Autism into Art: A Handicap Transfigured," in *High-Functioning Individuals with Autism,* E. Schopler and G. B. Mesibov, eds. (New York: Plenum Press, 1992).

———. "Elly and the Right to Education," in *Contemporary Issues in Special Education,* R. E. Schmid, J. Moneypenny, and R. Johnston, eds. (New York: McGraw-Hill, 1977).

———. "Growing Out of Autism," in *Autism in Adolescents and Adults,* E. Schopler and G. B. Mesibov, eds. (New York: Plenum Press, 1983).

———. *The Siege: A Family's Journey into the World of an Autistic Child.* Boston: Little, Brown, 2001. First published in 1967 as *The Siege: The First Eight Years of an Autistic Child;* reissued in 1982 with an epilogue, "Fifteen Years After."

———. "Social Growth in Autism: A Parent's Perspective," in *Social Behavior in Autism,* E. Schopler and G. B. Mesibov, eds. (New York: Plenum Press, 1986).

Park, David. "Operant Conditioning of a Speaking Autistic Child," *Journal of Autism and Childhood Schizophrenia,* vol. 4, no. 2 (1974), pp. 189–191.

Park, David, and Philip Youderian. "Light and Number: Ordering Principles in the World of an Autistic Child," *Journal of Autism and Childhood Schizophrenia,* vol. 4, no. 4 (1974), pp. 313–323.

Useful Addresses

United States

Autism Research Institute, 4182 Adams Avenue, San Diego, CA 92116. Tel: (619) 281-7165; Web site: **www.autism.com/ari**.

Autism Services Center, 605 Ninth Street, P.O. Box 507, Huntington, WV 25710–0507. Tel: (304) 525-8014; Web site: **www.autismservices.com**; e-mail: **autismservices@aol.com**.

Autism Society of America, 7910 Woodmont Avenue, Suite 300, Bethesda, MD 20814-3015. Tel: (301) 657-0881; (800) 328-8476; Web site: **www. autism-society.org**. Founded by parents in the days when parents were under suspicion, the society now includes thousands of parents, teachers, and physicians nationwide. With chapters in every state, it is the parent's and teacher's best resource, and should be every professional's first recommendation.

MAAP Services, Inc., P.O. Box 524, Crown Point, IN 46308. Tel: (219) 662-1311; Web site: **www.maapservices.org**.

Overseas

Autism-Europe, Avenue E. Van Becelaere 26B, bte 21, B-1170 Brussels, Belgium. Tel: +32 (0)2 675 72 70; e-mail: **autisme.europe@arcadis.be**; Web site: **www.autismeurope.arc.be**.

National Autistic Society, 393 City Road, London EC1V-1NG, United Kingdom. Tel: Main switchboard, +44 (0)20 7833 2299; helpline: +44 (0)870 600 8585; e-mail: **nas@nas.org.uk**. Its Web site, **www.oneworld. org/autism_uk,** provides a link to a wide variety of sites, including international organizations and informational sites. The society maintains a listing of autism societies all over the world. Travelers who contact these will find autism opens the door to shared experience that crosses every border.

Source Notes

Chapter 1: Introductory

1. The words are from my earlier book about Jessy, *The Siege: The First Eight Years of an Autistic Child,* originally published by Little, Brown in 1967. It was reissued in 1982 with an epilogue, "Fifteen Years After." It is being issued in 2001 as *The Siege: A Family's Journey into the World of an Autistic Child.* (The quoted passage is on page 3.)

2. Bruno Bettelheim, *The Empty Fortress: Infantile Autism and the Birth of the Self* (New York: Free Press, 1967), p. 125.

3. Leo Kanner, "Autistic Disturbances of Affective Contact" (1943), in *Classic Readings in Autism,* A. M. Donnellan, ed. (New York: Teachers College, Columbia University, 1985), p. 50. Kanner spoke at a meeting of the National Society for Autistic Children, July 17–19, 1969.

4. Clifford Geertz, "Learning with Bruner," *New York Review of Books,* April 10, 1997.

Chapter 2: "That is not sound"

1. Lorna Wing, "The Relationship Between Asperger's Syndrome and Kanner's Autism," in *Autism and Asperger Syndrome,* Uta Frith, ed. (Cambridge: Cambridge University Press, 1991), p. 111.

2. Ibid., p. 109.

3. *Diagnostic and Statistical Manual of Mental Disorders,* fourth edition (DSM IV) (Washington, D.C.: American Psychiatric Association, 1994).

4. *NAARRATIVE: Newsletter of the National Alliance for Autism Research,* no. 3 (fall 1998).

5. Ibid., no. 6 (summer 2000).

Chapter 3: "When the time comes"

1. Kanner, op. cit., p. 43.

2. Ibid., pp. 43–44.

3. Frith, in *Autism and Asperger Syndrome,* p. 18.

4. Ibid., p. 19.

5. Kanner, op. cit., p. 37.
6. Eric Courchesne et al., "Recent Advances in Autism," in *Neurobiology and Infantile Autism,* H. Naruse and E. M. Ornitz, eds. (New York: Elsevier Science Publications, 1992), p. 115.

Chapter 4: "Guess what!"

1. Wing, op. cit., p. 95; Bryna Siegel, *The World of the Autistic Child: Understanding and Treating Autistic Spectrum Disorders* (New York: Oxford University Press, 1996), pp. 49–50.
2. See Paul's afterword in Jane Taylor McDonnell's *News from the Border: A Mother's Memoir of Her Autistic Son* (New York: Ticknor & Fields, 1993), pp. 373–375.

Chapter 5: "All different kind of days"

1. Lola Bogyo and Ronald Ellis, "Elly: A Study in Contrasts," in *The Exceptional Brain,* L. K. Obler and D. Fein, eds. (New York: Guilford Press, 1988), pp. 268–271. The authors have kept the pseudonym I used for Jessy in *The Siege*.
2. Ibid.
3. Ibid.
4. David Park and Philip Youderian, "Light and Number: Ordering Principles in the World of an Autistic Child," *Journal of Autism and Childhood Schizophrenia,* vol. 4, no. 4 (1974), pp. 315–318.
5. The quotations are from Frances Groves Dodd, unpublished journal, entries of October 20 and November 27, 1972.

Chapter 6: "When I ten, *that* minus one!"

1. For more on Jessy's slow road to a full school day, see C. C. Park, "Elly and the Right to Education," in *Contemporary Issues in Special Education,* R. E. Schmid, J. Moneypenny, and R. Johnston, eds. (New York: McGraw-Hill, 1977), pp. 34–37.
2. Bogyo and Ellis, op. cit., pp. 269–270. For more on Jessy's numbers, see Park and Youderian, "Light and Number."

Chapter 7: "The hangman hangs by the clothespin because of new politeness"

1. For one of these drawings of number people, see *The Siege,* 1982 or 2001 edition.

2. Uta Frith, *Autism: Explaining the Enigma* (Oxford: Basil Blackwell, 1989), p. 12; Frith, in *Autism and Asperger Syndrome,* p. 17.
3. "Lewis and Boucher (1988) have shown that autistic children's pretense is unimpaired relative to controls when the play is 'instructed,' that is, when the children are told what to pretend." Gregory Currie, "Simulation-Theory, Theory-Theory, and Evidence from Autism," in *Theories of Theories of Mind,* P. Carruthers and P. K. Smith, eds. (Cambridge: Cambridge University Press, 1996), p. 251.
4. Wing, op. cit., p. 109.

Chapter 8: "The sky is purple-black"
1. Stephen Wiltshire, *Floating Cities;* foreword by Oliver Sacks (New York: Summit Books, 1991).
2. Ernest C. Pascucci, exhibition catalog for "A World of a Different Color — The Paintings of Jessica Park," The Bookcellar Café, Cambridge, Massachusetts, February 29–May 1, 1992 (unpublished).

Chapter 9: "Because can tell by the face"
1. Christopher Gillberg, "Clinical and Neurological Aspects of Asperger Syndrome in Six Family Studies," in Frith, ed., *Autism and Asperger Syndrome,* p. 132.
2. Courchesne et al., op. cit., p. 120.

Chapter 10: "I guess Darth Vader learned from consequences! Like me!"
1. For more, see D. Park, "Operant Conditioning of a Speaking Autistic Child," *Journal of Autism and Childhood Schizophrenia,* vol. 4, no. 2 (1974), pp. 189–191.
2. J. R. Cautela and J. Groden, *Relaxation: A Comprehensive Manual for Adults, Children, and Children with Special Needs* (Champaign, Ill.: Research Press, 1978).

Chapter 11: "Guess what! Some of the people at work are my friends!"
1. Reproduced in *The Siege,* 1982 and 2001 editions.
2. C. C. Park, "Growing Out of Autism," in *Autism in Adolescents and Adults,* E. Schopler and G. B. Mesibov, eds. (New York: Plenum, 1983), p. 294.

3. The whole episode can be seen in "Rage for Order," the hour-long section on autism from the BBC's series on Dr. Oliver Sacks, *The Mind Traveller,* shown in 1996 on PBS (Rosetta Pictures for the British Broadcasting Company, directed by Christopher Rawlence).

Picture Credits and Copyright Acknowledgments

Picture Credits

Howard Levitz, TGL Photoworks, Williamstown, MA: All photographs in the color insert; photographs on pages 1, 117, and 127.

David Park: Photographs on pages 106, 107, and 128.

Rosalie Winard: All photographs in the black-and-white insert; photographs on pages iii and 105.

Copyright Acknowledgments

Picture Credits and Copyright Acknowledgments

Autism in Adolescents and Adults, Plenum Press, 1983; "Social Growth in Autism: A Parent's Perspective," in E. Schopler and G. B. Mesibov, eds., *Social Behavior in Autism,* Plenum Press, 1986; and "Autism into Art: A Handicap Transfigured," in E. Schopler and G. B. Mesibov, eds., *High-Functioning Individuals with Autism,* Plenum Press, 1992.

Passages in chapter 3 from Eric Courchesne et al., "Recent Advances in Autism," reprinted from H. Naruse and E. M. Ornitz, eds., *Neurobiology and Infantile Autism,* Elsevier Science Publications, 1992. Reprinted by permission of Elsevier Science.

Passages in chapters 5 and 6 from Lola Bogyo and Ronald Ellis, "Elly: A Study in Contrasts," reprinted from L. K. Obler and D. Fein, eds., *The Exceptional Brain* (Guilford Press, 1988). Reprinted by permission of the publisher.

Passages in chapter 5 from David Park and Philip Youderian, "Light and Number: Ordering Principles in the World of an Autistic Child," reprinted by permission from *Journal of Autism and Childhood Schizophrenia,* vol. 4, no. 4 (1974).

Passage in Appendix I reprinted with permission from *Diagnostic and Statistical Manual of Mental Disorders,* fourth edition. Copyright 1994 American Psychiatric Association.

Made in the USA
Middletown, DE
11 July 2024